THE GAP IN THE MIDDLE

HOW TO BE AN ENTREPRENEUR OR SMALL
BUSINESS WHO SELLS TO CORPORATE AND
GOVERNMENT ORGANISATIONS

CAROL DEVENEY

To Bev Good luck in
your corporate
journey.

Carol

authors
AND CO.

CONTENTS

DEDICATION

To Ellen and Jim who taught me I could do anything I set my mind to and made it a self fulfilling prophecy.

1

INTRODUCTION

I f you are in business but haven't yet secured a regular flow of work from other businesses, corporate or government organisations, then welcome, dear reader, because you are where I began this story.

I bet you have a great product or service that you know works. It solves problems, brings joy or improves the world. If you could just get it into the right place with the right level of demand, then you could make money with less effort, more consistently... or at least with less stress of worrying where the next sale will come from.

Imagine how much time you could spend improving what you offer if you spent less time worrying about where that next customer is coming from. That energy, diverted in a positive way, is like a super fuel for entrepreneurs.

So, if that is the case, why are you spending so much time focusing on the next sale, worrying who is coming next to buy and looking over at those with regular corporate contracts and thinking 'it's all right for them'?

It probably is all right for them. It's not perfect. They do still have to think about the next order and the next contract. However, if they are working with corporates, they likely have a shorter essential turnover time between customers. By that, I mean the value of the work is likely higher and the length of time they are engaged in it longer. So rather than selling one widget at £1 to 4000 customers, one at a time, they sold £1000 of widgets to 4 customers. Each sale takes time, so the reduction in selling time, cost to acquire each customer and transaction time is reduced, even if the sale price was exactly the same.

What is so special about these others who have those contracts that you don't? Shall I share with you what I learned in over 20 years of corporate work on both sides of those contracts? What is so different is... absolutely nothing. Not a thing. Like everyone else in the world, they are no better and no worse than you are.

What they had is also the same as you. They had something to offer that they believed corporates needed. Just like you.

What they did? Now that is different. And it is something that you can exactly replicate. They took what they had to the corporate marketplace and they offered it to corporates. The joyful news is that if you have the right offer to sell, you are going to read this book, follow the method and do exactly the same as 'them'.

If you are selling services to a corporate market, you are selling business-to-business instead of business-to-consumer. It is likely that your rates are higher in business-to-business sales and whilst you may have some additional overheads, you are still likely to be making more profit per sale.

Corporate work allows you to create an ongoing relationship with multiple people at once. Consider if you sell training or coaching. You probably make one sale per person. They may come back and buy again and again from you, one transaction and one service at a time. No one is ever going to say 'that training session is awesome; I would like to buy two of them for myself next time and be twice as trained'.

Now, if you are selling to corporates, they are likely to be buying that coaching or training for multiple people in their company, so every piece of repeat business can again be a single transaction with multiple sales of your service. If it works well in one team or one department, they may also come back with new orders for a wider audience.

People with regular corporate work can start to see exponential growth in their business once they establish their business in that field.

So why is it 'them' and not you?

Perhaps you think they have a better network than you. They know who to talk to, when the contracts will come out and crucially, who needs what and when.

Maybe you had a look at working with corporates and got put off by the size and scale of some of the organisations who are your target market. I have worked in companies of 40,000 and 65,000. That is a small town. Who would even consider walking round an entire town asking everyone and trying to find the person who might want to buy anything from training to toasters? Surely that is a fool's errand?

Do you look at these faceless behemoths and wonder where you even start? There is no way in, over or under. At that point, you just go around and carry on your business-to-consumer work.

If that wasn't daunting enough, maybe the endless paperwork you imagine stacked up, just waiting to deter you from ever securing work, is putting you off. I mean, no one really likes paperwork, do they? It's killing trees, frustrating entrepreneurs and.... paper cuts – the worst!

Even if you had a way in and knew where to start, and who to speak to and what they even want that you offer, maybe you feel like if you got there, you wouldn't belong.

Isn't that our biggest fear? Every single one of us. It's not spiders or paperwork or no one buying our stuff. It is rejection. People looking right at us and making it clear that we are not of their tribe or herd. We do not belong.

This is actually a very rational fear. Humans are tribal and our very survival used to depend on remaining in the tribe. Those deep-rooted fears were meant to save us from being eaten by tigers or starving when we were too sick to hunt or gather. Great back then, but not so useful when it prevents us pitching our fine products and services in boardrooms because we are paralysed at the thought of rejection.

If you look at the corporate world or the reception of government organisations and think that you don't belong; if you think you wouldn't fit it in or that those steel and glass walls are not for the likes of you, then I want to let you into a secret.

Behind those walls are humans. Just plain humans. In all their wonderful, diverse forms. And every single one of them has those same primal fears as you.

Not one of them was born wearing a suit. I've checked and there are no recorded births of babies born wearing a suit. None of them were delivered straight to the boardroom or a corporate office. Every single one of them got there the way you are going to. And this book is going to help you get there. You just might not be in there 9-5 like they are.

By getting to know what your space in there is, getting comfortable with it and practising some techniques to help you feel like you are confident doing business with business, you will get there.

This book is going to take you through every one of those fears and dismantle them enough for you to prove to yourself that you belong. You won't win every contract but it won't feel like the end of the world.

You will find spaces and places and companies where you do not want to belong. They will not share your values or be a good buyer for your offer. You will make a list of those and forget about working with them. They won't occupy any more headspace. It is not that you are not for them but they are not for you. Ruling out a place on that basis feels a lot more comfortable than feeling rejected by them.

If you want to understand how you can be small and work with the big companies...

If you are a business owner who really wants to sell to other businesses or large organisations...

If you look at other people who do that all the time and want the same for you...

If you wish that you could pitch to big business and corporates, securing large contracts that give you some security in your business...

If you see other people secure corporate contracts and there is a part of you that thinks 'it should have been my product. Maybe next year', then when next year comes, the problem seems just as big and intangible and the solution seems further away...

This book is for you.

Do you know in your heart of hearts that your product or service really deserves a big audience?

Have you had the occasional piece of corporate work but feel it was a bit of a one-hit wonder and you don't know how to repeat that?

Do you really know that it works? In your heart of hearts, do you feel that what you make or what you offer is good enough for the corporate audience but you just don't know how to land it with them?

Do you think it would be great to have corporates knocking on your door with repeat business, year after year, but when you think about how to actually achieve that, it just seems too over-whelming?

Are there people around you who encourage you to go for it and wonder why you haven't got that one life-changing contract yet? Or perhaps it's your dark secret. You know it but you can't say it out loud in case everyone points out that you don't belong, or that no one will buy it. Maybe it could be worse. You could be a massive success and everyone buys. I mean, who wants to be wealthy and successful?

If any of this sounds like you, then this book is going to help you sell your goods or services to corporate organisations. I will take you from wondering whether you really could get into corporates to not only knowing that you can, but knowing that you will.

Let me tell you why you will. It is because corporates really want you to. You can read that again if you want, it will still say the same thing. And it's true. They not only want you to sell to them. They need you to sell to them.

Most large corporate and government organisations are driven by targets and objectives. They are set, planned, tracked and measured. You probably knew that. **But did you know that many of them have a target to work with small and medium sized businesses?**

Well, let's rest a moment in collective shock. I spend so much of my time inside corporate organisations that I am still shocked when I tell this to solopreneurs, microbusinesses, small businesses and even medium-sized businesses and they tell me they didn't know.

So, let's look at the position. Large companies are *under pressure* to work with small and medium enterprises (SMEs) and have targets to do so.

SMEs want the security and rates of working with corporates and government organisations.

Neither realises how much they want and need each other. Both sides tell me their barriers to working together more often, and that, my friends, is 'The Gap in the Middle'.

I am target driven and I would say that is the norm in most corporate organisations at a senior level.

In over 20 years of working in corporates, some years, the only target I did not hit was the number of SMEs I worked with. Can you imagine the number of target-driven people sitting there, ready for you to help them meet that target?

The UK government alone has a target that for every £3 spent, £1 will be with an SME. The original date was 2020. The date got moved to 2022. You can figure out why, right? Because no one was hitting that target.

Isn't it time you were offering your products or services to the corporate market and helping close that gap?

Large companies are huge consumers of products and services and you are the oil that keeps the cogs in the behemoth running.

When you have secured your first corporate deal, you will be well on the way to securing more corporate work. The first one will be the toughest and after that, you'll be able to repeat your success, partly because you will know that you can do it, partly because you will have a systematic method to do so and you will believe that you belong at those corporate tables.

This book takes you through my proven method that I used when I left working in large corporate organisations to set up my own international consultancy. I took all the steps that I'm going to ask you to take.

I took all the steps that I'm going to share with you and I have a multi-6-figure business. I have clients in 8 countries on 3 continents. I have a stable flow of work, called a pipeline, and multiple repeat clients.

Here is my big promise to you. You can identify something that you're going to be able to sell and know how to do that. I've been here and I know what you can achieve or become by doing this.

You will know why it is that you want to be working with corporates. You will know what you're going to say, where to start, who to start with and you'll be able to avoid being a one-hit wonder.

I will give you practical advice that will take you closer to your goal.

I will teach you how I did it. I used my trademarked strategy called The Corporate Method. You will learn how to apply each step in The Corporate Method by the end of this book.

My 9-step method that you can replicate is:

Confirm your why

Outline your vision

Research your ideal clients or industry

Proposal definition

Overcome your doubts

Refine your strategy

Articulate your offer

Take it to market

Ethical entertaining

Let's not wait any longer. I'm a massive action taker, which has been a really successful attribute working in corporate. People who get things done get things done. I invite you now to turn the page. Follow my steps to getting into working with corporates and closing that gap in the middle.

2

THE GAP IN THE MIDDLE

For years, I have heard entrepreneurs say that they are too small to work with the big companies. I knew this wasn't true but I also knew it was their truth. That is not some kind of 1984 doublespeak! What I mean is that their perception has become their reality. The fact that they believe they are too small to play big has become a self-fulfilling reality.

I want it to stop. I know so many entrepreneurs who would be amazing working with corporates, some whom are just a few steps away from being ready. I want you to feel that you can do, be and have the options you choose.

Before I could help with changing that perception, I knew I had to understand what was driving it. Why do so many self-sufficient, self-reliant, creative, problem solving, amazing entrepreneurs think that corporate contracts are not theirs for the taking.

I mean, these are the people grabbing the world by the impolite-to-mention-at-a-dinner-table body parts and creating their own futures from their dreams. How could these folk, who take the risk of not having that regular paycheck and all the lovely things that go with being employed (support teams, not being your own IT, plumber, estate agent, ops manager, HR directors and so on till exhaustion), and creating value, jobs and income, think anything was beyond them?

'If you can dream it, you can do it' may be an easy mantra but we are talking about people dreaming it, doing it, dreaming bigger, doing bigger and doing it, often in the beginning anyway, with limited resources and all the fears and risks that go with self employment.

So how could these doers of deeds be thinking that anything less than the world is not theirs for the taking?

I am a naturally curious person and my parents fostered that curiosity. I was not brought up to believe that I had to accept how the world was in an unquestioning way. I was brought up to believe that you seek to understand and that you can also drive change where you see that which is unfair, unjust or just plain old wrong.

This has served me well in life and work and is something I have instilled in my own child. A word of caution is that you may also spend a lot of time quietly kicking yourself as your child demands unlimited answers and justifications from you (that was not in the plan). You may also have to explain to teachers why they are not a perfect sponge, soaking up the education being carefully curated for them and that occasionally, maybe they could accept some of that without the questions!

I digress. The point is I needed to get really curious about what was going on with entrepreneurs excluding themselves from what could often be the best rate they would get for their work.

When I left the corporate world, I knew one of the things I would miss would be being part of something. That feeling of belonging to a community of people with a united purpose, doing something that really matters in the world.

I think if you haven't ever worked in corporates, you might not think that is one of the benefits. You might see that faceless behemoth and think 'that looks soulless'. The veneer may be soulless, but corporates are populated with people. Like every large group of people, that means there is an average and there are outliers. So, there will be a group of mostly fine folk. Then there will be some people who are just totally and utterly your people, your tribe, your folk whatever you want to call it.

You will have the fact that you work together as your common denominator, but then you will have a million more things that bind you together. Then there are the folk that might be fine, but you and they just don't gel. You are not for each other. In a big company, that is ok. If you need to work together, you do, but you are not going to be buddies. Neither of you have a problem with that as you've already got all those people who are.

There are also a handful of abominable people. People whose values and behaviours you just abhor. People who you are embarrassed to work for the same company as. To protect the guilty and save on a lot of litigation, we shall leave those people unspoken about in this book. Also, why give oxygen to their fire? They are abominable, after all.

Leaving corporates to be self employed is like leaving your home-town. If you go back, a lot of people will be the same and be doing the same. You will love that familiarity as it is warm, cosy and reassuring. But you will be different and there will be parts of you that no longer fit the same. There will be discussions that you are never going to have because of the changes that have occurred in you.

If you leave corporate, you will keep some of those friendships. Many people leave corporate and, like me, their contacts from corporate become clients. That is a great way to get into corporate. What you are not going to do is meet up with those folks and tell them about the business side of running your business. You cannot discuss the ups and downs of your other clients with them. You are also not going to get into some of the empathetic discussions about the personal journey of being an entrepreneur that you absolutely need to do with other entrepreneurs.

I knew that when I left corporate, so I started to build a new network. An alternative community of entrepreneurs. People who had lived or were living my new path.

I knew that I would need those people - not to do things for me, but to be part of their community, to still feel a part of something bigger than me.

I did that in several ways. One of which led me to write this book.

What became clear quite quickly was that the barrier between entrepreneurs working with corporates came down to 3 things. The gap, the mindset, and the how to.

The first thing was the gap in the middle.

A lot of entrepreneurs were not aware that corporates not only wanted them, but needed them.

I've said that a corporate organisation is like a small town, some are even more like cities. What I mean by that comparison is in terms of how many people populate them. I work in transport in several continents, so my geography is pretty good. Also, I am fascinated by maps, travel books and social geography. I don't like to boast too much but I did recently treat myself to 'Transit Maps of the World' and it is the visual and intellectual treat I thought it would be. It has also become a bit of a wish list of transit journeys.

So, that geography nerdiness means I can easily find a city to turn my anecdote into a statistic.

For example, St David's in Wales is the United Kingdom's smallest city, with a population of 1600. The United States has lots of tiny cities, from the desert city of Joshua Tree in California, population 7414, to the Alaskan city of Akhoik at 70.

Canada has made a sensible provision that to be a city you must swell your numbers to 10,000. However, that city status, once conferred, is not revoked if your numbers drop below 10,000 for any reason so they, of course, have plenty of depopulated cities that fall below that.

But I am not playing fast and loose with the semantics to prove a point. The fact is that many sizeable cities such as:

Flint, Michigan, United States

Bath, United Kingdom

Whitby, Ontario, Canada

Bendigo, Australia

All have a population around 100,000. Decent sized cities.

Now let's look at some corporate organisations. Starting with transport, Network Rail, who owned and managed the UK rail infrastructure, had 38,000 people directly employed by them in 2018, with another 100,000 working in their supply chain. In the financial services sector, Lloyds employ 65,000 and J.P Morgan employ 270,000 people.

Why is that relevant to entrepreneurs who want to work in corporates? Well, it is because all those city sized populations have needs. Massive needs. Needs that go beyond the obvious. Sure, 270,000 people in a financial services organisation will need finance related products. They also need all the things that fuel and service those people, year in, year out. Can you imagine how much milk gets poured into the coffee of 270,000 people? What about their training needs, printing paper, ink, lease cars, accommodation when travelling, Christmas gifts, desk diaries, counselling, physiotherapy, event venues, photo shoots, communications? If I start to write the list of resources consumed by an organisation which either makes or builds things, then I will have completed my word count for this book, but it will be rather dull which is not my aim despite my penchant for sharing geography factoids with you.

The point is, corporates are consumers of goods, products, services, materials and work on an immense scale. They are under constant pressure to keep their costs down. That means they cannot have standing armies of people who might possibly deliver every service or product they might ever need. No, they have staff doing the essentials and a supply chain ready to provide everything else when it is needed.

You really **are** the oil that keeps the behemoth cogs turning.

There is huge opportunity for entrepreneurs there just on the scale alone. That, my friends, is not the whole story. Yes, there is massive demand (amazing news, right?) but there is more.

I have mentioned before that in the UK, the government has been pushing the organisations it funds to work with SMEs to spend a minimum of a third of its expenditure that way.

In the US and Canada, the beloved Mom and Pop stores are etched in the national conscience but what about policy? In the US, there is again a policy level statement to encourage spending at the rate of around a third with SMEs.

In Canada, most provinces have the same level of commitment at around 33% of their spend aiming to be with SMEs.

In Australia it is sitting at an average 30% target too.

All of them are falling short. Whilst they are all government targets, remember that they do a lot of business with large corporates and encourage them to replicate these targets in their supply chains.

For people with businesses like you and me, this is great news. Everyone wants to do business with us and is being set targets to encourage them to do so.

When I worked in corporate, I was always working to targets to work with SMEs. And you know what? Sometimes I tried really hard and it just didn't happen.

I would meet or find people who wanted to work with us. Their eyes would widen when I talked about the monetary values of the contracts available. They would be keen, we would flirt with the idea, we would court each other... but often we never got beyond a first date.

Sometimes it would get further but then, as we started to get serious, they would cool off. They would tell me it wasn't me; it was them. We've all heard that before, haven't we?

I would love to say I followed up intensely. Asked all the great questions to understand what put them off. The reality is that I didn't. I was busy and sometimes I was even just busy being busy. There were plenty of tried and tested suppliers happy to take on those contracts when a newer player baulked at the hurdles.

So, even though at times I wanted new blood to either keep things interesting or to make sure costs stayed competitive, I would end up back with the same old suppliers.

Then I would hear the same words from small business that I hear now when I tell them about the world of possibility and financial security that they are missing out on:

'They always just go with the same old suppliers, the 'Usual Suspects'

I hear this a lot about corporate work. I see this happen and I hear solopreneurs and small businesses say that they feel disheartened that they will put in a lot of effort for no return. With enough to do in their business, it just doesn't seem worth it when the Usual Suspects end up winning the work anyway.

I'll tell you a story about why I ended up with the Usual Suspect when really what I wanted was the Next Bright New Thing.

I was a Head of Profession for a large corporate. One of my roles was to put on an annual conference event over 2-3 days for everyone in my profession. That is 350 people who want to be educated, challenged, entertained, informed, raised up, praised, feel part of a community and go back to their very challenging day jobs feeling like it is a little easier or more worthwhile than before the conference.

I would be thinking about next year's conference 2 days after that year's finished. Every year I wanted it to be better. One of the things I would do is go to relevant conferences and watch other speakers. I'd be shopping for who would be great for my profession.

One year, I attended an industry conference and I saw a speaker who blew my socks off. I knew that the profession would love them.

This had happened the year before at a previous conference and I approached the speaker, who we will call Andrew, and asked him to get in touch. Andrew got in touch, did what he had to do, and he had just stormed my conference. In fact, Andrew still works with that company as a major client even though I have long moved on.

So, at this point I am delighted. This is going to be amazing for the profession. Two years in a row, we will bring them something so useful, so tangible and something they can deploy right away to make their job easier.

I approach the speaker. This speaker is called Bob. Bob and I have a great chat. I tell him who I work for and Bob says he has always wanted to work with them as a client. I give Bob my details and suggest he gets in touch as I would like him to be at our conference next September.

That's nine months away but I suggest we speak soon as, if he has never worked with us, it can take a bit of time to get him approved as a supplier.

Bob emails me in August.

I have already issued the conference invites, the agenda is published, I have requested materials from speakers. I have bought my outfit and written my own speech. We are good to go.

Worse news for Bob - I have filled his spot with a Usual Suspect. A great Usual Suspect - reliable, interesting... but not blow your socks off awesome, like Bob.

I can tell he is disappointed but the reality of getting him onto our approved supplier list, into contract and working within a month is not only unrealistic but would rely on me pulling every favour I had from the procurement teams. Favours from procurement teams are like Genie's wishes, you do not waste these!

Procurement is just a fancy word used in corporates to mean everything involved in buying goods, services and works.

Bob is still blowing your socks off awesome, but now he is offering to speak at my conference for free for exposure. It's a

THE GAP IN THE MIDDLE

smart move but exposure doesn't pay the bills. I suggest Bob gets onto our supplier list and think about next year.

By the following year, I had moved on to another company, so I don't know if Bob got onto that list. I suspect not because I hear about and see the work that Andrew does all the time being praised by that company, but I never hear Bob's name.

I sometimes wonder how Bob sits easy with a desire to work with that company for all those years yet doesn't follow through on the necessary actions.

In a few years, Andrew will have become a Usual Suspect whilst Bob will still be on the speaker circuit, promoting his brilliant idea without securing contracts.

When I left corporate, I had the time to reflect on those hurdles that prevent entrepreneurs like you working with corporates. I had time to ask entrepreneurs. That is when I learned that not only is there demand from corporates to work with SMEs, but also there is a desire from entrepreneurs to work with corporates. But there is a big Gap in the Middle.

That is what this book and my work aim to close.

So, my first promise to you is this: they want you, they need you.

The second hurdle I heard was a lot of phrases that all come under the category of mindset.

- I'm just not corporate
- I hated working in corporate
- They won't want someone like me
- I don't fit in there

- I don't look, sound, think, dress [add your own self-bashing words here] like them
- I'm not enough
- I'm too much
- They are too much
- What if I get the work but can't meet the expectation?
- No one would pay me that day rate for what I can do
- The market is already too crowded (this one makes me want to weep, remembering all those missed targets)

I hear so much negative self-talk when I ask people how they feel about getting corporate work.

You might read that list and think 'Yes, that is me. That is my very good reason for not doing the work'. You can close this book safe that you have been seen and that I have validated your fears and thus, this is over for you.

You do not need to step out of your comfort zone and into the growth zone which we all know to be uncomfortable, even though it leads to change, improvement and success. So, you can stay in comfort and mosey along.

But what about if you don't?

What about if we take every single one of those fears and move you to a position of safety in each one? What if I told you that most people who do have lucrative, sustained corporate work all had some of those fears at some point? What if I promised you that your fears are trying to protect you but that you can move safely beyond those fears? You can move beyond them and eventually look back at them and laugh in their face because they no longer hurt you or hold you.

Think about what you will achieve when you have moved beyond them. I don't like to say overcome them because it sets up fears like a physical wall in your mind. Suddenly, you start to see yourself needing grappling hooks, battering rams, intense marine style training and immense effort to get over them. It sets them up even bigger.

When really, they are thoughts and emotions that are trying to help you. To keep you safe from harm, from failure, from rejection. Those things all suck, and your primitive brain is doing great work at trying to protect you.

You know what though? You don't need it. You need to systematically look at each fear with your rational, intellectual brain. You need to assess it and set it aside and move right on to winning those contracts and doing that work. Taking your place with those corporate companies who need you, who are desperate for you to be the oil in their cogs, to keep them turning.

In Chapter 7 - Overcome Your Doubts, we will talk about overcoming doubts in more detail. I will share emotional and practical advice to move you forward in a way that will be a mix of comfort and stretch, with only a slight dose of panic from time to time.

I already know you can do hard stuff. I also know you can do hard stuff even when you doubt yourself. How do I know that? I know that because you run your own business. Whether you have a solo gig you run from your bed or a medium-sized business you have someone else run for you. Whatever size your business is, you have already chosen to tread a challenging path.

I suspect people tell you that they really admire you for running your own show and you bat it off as if anyone could do it. They could do it. You **are** doing it.

If you can do that, you can do this. I'm not saying it is easy. I will be the first to admit that some things are more readily suited to a corporate audience than others. If your product or service needs a bit of adaptation, it may take longer or it may take more steps, but you can do it.

Please do it because it is the only way the gap in the middle will ever close. You are important in the supply chain of corporate and government contracts. They need you. They want you and they are incentivised to work with you.

You are also going to have to fill out the paperwork. You can do this on your own or you can get help. It is less complicated than it first seems. Partly because most companies will be asking you the same things in a different way or format. It also gets easier the more you do it, as you learn the terminology and the format.

You do not need to be huge to work with the big companies. You can be medium, small or micro and still work with the big corporates. This book is going to help you do that.

The third hurdle was how to do it. The actual practical steps. One after the other. How do you construct a strategy and a plan with a series of actions that you can follow to get your first contracts, right through to how do you get a regular pipeline of work? This book will walk you through those steps.

Every time you start to think that maybe you can't do it, maybe the steps are for others or people who are smarter, thinner, younger, older, funnier, more serious, healthier, taller, shorter or whatever adjective you use as a measuring stick for success, I will remind you that these steps are for you. And they are for you, now. Right as you are. Not some future idealistic you.

You know why? Because corporate organisations are full of people who also have flaws. Some are obvious and some are deep-down, hidden fears that aren't real except in the minds of the individual. So, they are as flawed as you and as wonderful as you. So, let us not hang around for future you. The only certainty we have about future you is that you will be older.

You may have heard the phrase Corporate Social Responsibility. Lovely little corporate phrase that may well mean zilch, zero to anyone outside of corporate. The concept is really a corporate response to accusations of big companies sucking up all the wealth and resources in the world and giving nothing back. A rejection, if you like, of the values of the faceless behemoths.

The idea of Corporate Social Responsibility is basically that the big corporates will play nice with the rest of us. They will make commitments about how they treat the planet, communities they impact upon, their own people and other businesses.

They often have these statements on their websites and they are a good source for you to look at and see if they have statements in their Corporate Social Responsibility policy about working either with local suppliers or SMEs. For a while, Corporate Social Responsibility was the in phrase. Some companies, including my own, have widened their thinking to have a sustainability policy that incorporates Corporate Social Responsibility.

Now we have looked at why they want to work with you. We have also established that you are a fine specimen of a human who either believes that you can work with them or you are willing to suspend any elements of disbelief until Chapter 7 - Overcome Your Doubts.

What we are going to explore next is why you want to work with them.

3

CONFIRM YOUR WHY

When I say confirm your why, I mean more than one thing, but 'confirm your whys' is a grammatical error that I cannot bear to bring forth in the world, even for such a noble reason as helping you achieve your dreams.

I am a big fan of the methodology of using 5 whys. I use it often in corporate contracts for certain types of work. One is when doing a lesson learned, looking into when or where something went wrong, or something went right. I will give you one guess as to the balance of how often a lesson learned focuses on what went right versus what went wrong!

Did you guess more on the 'what when wrong' by a factor of about 100-1? Correct. Either way, rarely is the first answer to why something went wrong or well the full story. That is not to say it is a cover up answer, but that there is often more complexity in a problem than you get when you ask why the first time.

Another time I use it is when planning change. Change management and projects have been my career for decades now. What I know is that until you thoroughly understand why you are making the change and what the benefits are, you cannot convince anyone else to join in the change journey in any sort of convinced way.

So, we will why our whys. Can I bear that grammar? Let's see if it survives the edit.

There are a few whys for you to consider.

Firstly, why do you want to work with corporates?

Brainstorm this one. Write down every idea that springs to mind. Then you are going to apply 5 why questioning to each answer on your brainstormed ideas. You will find that even some of the left field ones will have a deep-rooted reason somewhere.

I will give you some guidance here on the first one that is likely to come up so that you can see how you can apply the 5 whys questioning.

Let's say that you have written "make more money" or "work less hours" as one of the reasons you want to work with corporates. If you want to work less hours for a higher rate, that is perfectly fine. Fiscal reasons are perfectly acceptable reasons to want to work with corporates.

Still, dig a little deeper if that is your answer.

- Why do you want to work less and earn more?
- Why?
- Why is that important to you?

- Why?
- Why is that a goal?

This is about plumbing into the depths of your own mind and really getting clear on what is driving you. As humans, we are complex beings. My mother is a wise woman. There was a time when I was trying to comprehend the actions of someone who had behaved rather badly towards me and out of character for them. I have a degree and a post grad in business and leadership and years of post qualification experience working on frameworks, models and theories about human behaviours, so I was trying to look at it from all angles.

My mother pointed out that no matter how much we know about psychology and 4 box models, sometimes we can't even understand why we took a certain action of our own and we are inside our own mind. That stuck with me and I do think that this exercise helps us get a deeper understanding of what is in our subconscious mind as well as our conscious mind. It helps us understand more about motivation and when the going gets tough, you can more easily connect to that and remind yourself of why you are doing it.

Here is a word of caution. If everything that comes up in your 5 why questioning is about other people's expectation of you and nothing about what you want, then you must give some real consideration to whether you want this or others want this for you.

That is different from you want this but have some mindset fears and your best cheerleaders are driving you on because they believe in you. I am talking about if you cannot see any reason at all that you would want to do this. The only reasons coming up are about what other people want from you or for you.

If your parents want this for you and you abhor the idea but want to please them or allow them to live vicariously through you, then this is the not book you need to help you. Live your own dream; they had their life.

If your partner wants this and is pushing you because they can see a lifestyle change attached to it, but you abhor the thought of it, then hand them this book and get them to build a business that works with corporates.

If your dog wants this for you... Hang on. Your dog would never want you to do anything you don't want. Your dog would never want you to be unhappy. Actually, your dog might be a better cheerleader than anyone who wants you to do something that you are resisting so strongly. Good instincts, dogs.

It is important to dig into this deep because understanding your own motivation is vital. Whether it is that you want to see inside a corner office, or you have a product that will change lives if you can get it to mass market. Whatever your motivations, it won't be binary. The better you understand the reasons, the more you can use them to motivate yourself.

There is also a little mindset trick that I am going to teach you later that will help you whenever fear gremlins nibble at you. The trick relies on you knowing why you started all this in the first place.

Another reason you need to know why you are motivated to work with corporates is so that you can articulate it to the people

THE GAP IN THE MIDDLE

you want to work with, and the people you want to help get you to those people.

No one will massively object to you saying I want to make more money but if you have a more nuanced and personal answer, it will resonate more. Using the power of storytelling is something we will look at in the chapter called Articulate Your Offer. For now, it is enough to assess your motivations in depth.

Why now?

I want you to keep a note of this one particularly and at the point when you feel like maybe you shouldn't bother, maybe next year, maybe never or whenever those voices in your head try to divert you from this course, you will look at the "why now". Look at it and remind yourself that there is no time like now.

A good way to answer why now is to flip it and ask yourself why not now? Or if not now, when? I am going to point out to you that if you want to wait until you are less busy then you will also have to plan how and when you are going to be less busy as hope is not a scheduling tool.

Entrepreneurs rarely want to be less busy if it means dropping income. Working with corporates is going to make you more money in less time, once you have it up and running, so how are you going to create the time to do that? Even if you know that it will take 6 months of planning to execute, you can start to plan that now.

Why do you do what you do?

This is no time to be humble so let's get real here. Sometimes our ego can get in the way of us talking about our accomplishments. I know that you don't want to be boastful or a show off, but no one is going to buy into you without you dropping some of the self-effacing stuff and being able to confidently explain why you do what you do. You see, a huge part of why you do it is going to sell it to others.

If your reason why comes across as you have a mediocre level of talent in that area, your product is sort of, kind of ok and you want to do it because you can't think of anything better to occupy your time or generate an income, how do you think that lands?

In the days of the early Roman Empire, fish sellers would often call out 'stinking fish, stinking fish' even though their fish was freshly caught and delicious. It was not because they had stinking fish but because their product was taxed based on quality. This was to deter taxes and because customers knew that, it did not put them off buying.

Now, I am not saying our taxation systems are any more sophisticated, but I can tell you that too much self effacement or playing down of you or your product will sound like a 'stinking fish' call to customers in a world of saturation marketing, social media and brand awareness. And worse, because you are not taxed on quality, they really will think it stinks.

The other end of the scale is the in your face, I'm amazing; everything I touch turns to success or gold; my product is the only thing you need in your life and that is why I do this.

That might win round some people who get caught up in that energy, but it will not lead to a long-term pipeline of corporate contracts.

What you are going to do is find that middle ground.

- Why do you do what you do?
- Is it because you love it?
- Because you are great at it?
- Because you love the environment it lets you work in?
- Because you love the people?
- Because you love the results you see people get?
- Because you know that this product is unique, innovative or exceptional?
- Because you have created something that is at a price point new to the market – that can be low, mid or high end?

Ask Why 5 times to every one of your answers.

When you are working with corporates, they expect you to be able to say what you are good at with confidence and clarity. They will not feel awkward and neither should you. They are willing to exchange cash for what you are good at.

Here is another bonus: you don't have to be good at everything so you don't have to fake it to make it. You can genuinely tell them what you are good at and why you do it. For everything else, there will be someone else.

I am totally conformable, if a client asks me to do something, to say, 'I'm not a specialist in that so I could bring you someone better at it', then I reach out to my network and bring in someone who is. They either work via me or on their own. You know why? Because I know why I do what I do and I know that I am really good at it and I have a corporate pipeline of work based on that.

I do it for these whys (I know, I am stretching these plural whys, but bear with me):

- Because I am good at it
- Because I enjoy doing it well
- Because I am motivated by helping people, doing good work and by success
- Because I have a track record of doing it well that means I can charge prices that allow me to work the hours I want and earn the money I need for the lifestyle I enjoy.
- Because I want to offer a service that I couldn't find to buy when I was the person in corporate looking to buy it or access it.

Your why you do it might look quite different from mine. You are not me and that is perfectly fine - we are different people after all, and variety is so crucial in keeping life and the work interesting. If you know yours, you are in a great place to talk about it with confidence and the more that you do that, the more confident you will feel about it.

Why do corporates need what you have?

This could seem to be a simple answer. If you have a product or product range, you plan to get into retail and they make multiple sales of your product. But unless you have a brand-new, life-changing, never-been-thought-of-before product - I am talking on the scale of the wheel, sliced bread, medicine or hair straighteners (don't judge me) - then even getting your product into retail requires that you can answer that question. Products have competition from similar products and even from different products, as buyers have floor space and distribution volumes to consider. You don't see many signs above shop fronts that say 'come in we sell everything'.

Therefore, why your product? Is it better, cheaper, more luxurious, more sustainable, does the job better, locally made or sourced, shinier, matte-r, family business, handmade, new, old? Why should they care about what you want to sell them and why do they need it? Most importantly, why will their customers want to buy it from them?

This will form the basis of you taking your offer to market, so spend some time getting clear on it.

If you have a product or service that you already sell, ask people what they like about it and what they don't like about it. Are these factors that add to why corporates need it?

What else could it be? Do corporates regularly buy your service? If so, that is a very simple answer. You provide what they need. Supply and demand in its purest form. That might not be your competitive edge, but it is a good foundation. You have what they need, you are a small business, they have targets to meet on working with SMEs and you are ready to start to close that gap in the middle. This is a solid base.

If your monkey brain or gremlin is starting to say 'ah, but so do many others and they have a place in that gap, but you don't' then please mute that monkey or gremlin till Chapter 7. Let's stay focused on this part and we will come back to exorcising them later. There will be no moon rituals or celestial beings, but brain monkeys and gremlins will be harmed in that chapter. Not actual monkeys though because I love actual monkeys.

I find it very hard to see them in captivity because I want to set them free. I know that some zoos do conservation work, but I can't bear to see monkeys or anything else caged. I also know I cannot set them free and allow them to wander around Edinburgh or London, eating little kids and tearing the arms off adults, but the monkey brain encourages me to set them free. I digress... but a monkey digression is a good digression.

Bear with me... of bears I have many stories because I have lived in Canada, but I cannot indulge myself with a bear digression right after a monkey digression, so we go straight on here... bear with me and trust that this is for you. You will be part of closing the gap in the middle and you, my friend, are way more than filler. You are the delicious apricot jam in a Sachetorte, the cream in the Victoria Sponge and the jam in the donut.

Final why

Why should they do business with you?

Part of this is the whys (final plural why, I promise) that you have already considered. Now you wrap it up in that final bow of: why you?

There are lots of great books on finding your unique selling point and marketing that you can turn to. If you are running a business, especially a business-to-business one, then I highly recommend that you read business books regularly. For this why though you don't need to over complicate it.

- Why you?
- Do you have what they want and need, plus you help them meet SMEs targets?
- Are you the only person offering what you have?
- Are you the best?
- Are you local?
- Are you the most expensive?
- Cheapest?
- Best placed to help them?
- All the above?

Be prepared to answer why should we work with you? That is a very common question, and it is not a trick, so don't have a super fancy answer. Have a great answer, simply worded, that sets it out and positions your why at the heart of your answer.

Let me give you an example from my own business.

One of the services I provide is training and coaching for project sponsors. If a corporate, asks me why they should work with me I could say this:

I am the only business who internationally provides training for project sponsors, designed and delivered by project sponsors.

Now, that is on my website, in my marketing materials, it is part of my unique selling point and it is true.

Here is what I would say in that conversation.

I provide project sponsor training because when I was a project sponsor, I always wanted to learn ways to do my job better. I wanted to learn what good looked like and get the tools, knowledge and skills to be able to do it. It was never offered or available. Years later, when I was the Head of Sponsorship, I wanted to buy that training for over 300 people. The reason I couldn't was because it didn't exist. So, I set up a business which does provide it and I love bringing sponsors what I know they need and want.

Wordier? Yes. More powerful? Undoubtedly.

Can I say it in fewer words? Also, yes.

I started to provide the sponsor training that I couldn't buy anywhere in the world.

Sometimes you need that one sentence because you have limited time and need an impactful statement grounded in a why.

I also have the wordier version, which is a 30-minute journey through the difficulty of trying to succeed in a role which had no proper definition, success criteria or training path. That's for a niche audience of sponsors and is also in a different book!

So now we have covered why do it, why do it now, why you. Maybe it sounded quite philosophical and navel gazing to begin with, but I hope that you now have a sound foundation to move on with.

I have shared with you why corporates should work with me.

Why do I want to work with them at a deeper level?

Sunday morning meant two things when I was growing up: First was waking up at my Gran's house, as I spent most weekends there. Second was The Waltons at 10 am. We would get up on a Sunday morning. My Gran would make bacon sandwiches and me, my Gran and my brother would all settle in to watch The Waltons. We loved that show.

Nothing about The Waltons represented our reality. They lived in a hamlet in the Blue Ridge Mountains of Virginia. My gran lived in Possilpark, Glasgow. She lived in a street that became famous in the movie Trainspotting. The main character is abandoned in the street following a heroin overdose. The scene was filmed there only a few years after my Gran moved from that street. She moved mostly due to the prevalence of crime, fuelled by the heroin epidemic.

The happy family with traditional roles and a rosy view on getting through the Great Depression did not mirror our lives either. Poverty was rife on all sides of our family and no one was seeing nobility in it. My parents were the first generation to move away from that life and build something else for their family in any sustained way.

My Gran, widowed in her 50s, had never had a day in her life that resembled what we were watching. She had barely been able to enjoy being a mother, due to the poverty and domestic violence that accompanied my grandfather's alcoholism. I think the closest she ever got was me and my brother spending weekends with her. She loved that and she loved us and we all loved The Waltons. It was pure escapism and we revelled in it. We would talk about the characters as if they were part of our extended family.

And, of course, we said 'Goodnight, John Boy' at bedtime. We talked about how we would all go to Walton's Mountain as if that was a certainty. We would be as likely to fly to the moon to be honest. You see, although we talked about it, we knew it would never happen. Not only did people like us not up and fly to America but also, my Gran was terrified of flying. Despite the fact she liked to travel, nothing would ever get her on a plane. So, it was a pipedream.

It's a memory that has always stayed with me. It's an odd one as I'm not actually a huge TV fan. In fact, we don't even own a TV at home. I still love the Waltons though, deep in my heart. For years, I always wanted to visit that mountain.

When I was growing up, another huge part of life was books. My parents read to me every night and encouraged me to read. They didn't own a TV when I was younger and our house was filled with books and music instead.

What books did for me was transport me to places and on adventures beyond anything I could imagine. Except once you have read a lot, you CAN begin to imagine. You imagine yourself on those adventures. I would imagine myself going to all the places I read about. I would pour over my World Atlas and imagine going to Walton's Mountain, Knossos' Palace, The Hundred Acre Wood, all the places in London in the Paddington Stories, the New York skyline, the spot in Hampstead Heath where CS Lewis thought up the Lion, The Witch & The Wardrobe, Massachusetts, where the Little Women lived, Anne of Green Gables' home in Prince Edward Island, Canada, and on and on. The list of places I could imagine myself going was endless because it grew with every book I read. It still does.

The corporate career I have had, and the businesses I now run, continue to give me both the opportunity to travel and the means to include amazing adventures into my life. I am not particularly materialistic. I like nice things but I do not require a glut of them. Travel adventures have no limit and memories need no extra storage, however many you accumulate. And that is my why.

4

OUTLINE YOUR VISION

Now you know why you want to do it; I am going to take you through how to make it happen for you. Even better, how to make it happen again and again and again! Maybe you have made the odd sale, but you are not sure how or why. Maybe you make sales regularly, but the gaps between your contracts are too vast and you feel you want to improve the consistency. Maybe you have never sold to corporate and this is the start for you.

I don't want you to worry about where you are now because it does not make a difference to how you progress through the Corporate Method.

Wherever you are now is great (just like you are). We start from here and we go forward together.

I want you to start by thinking about what you want your business to look like when you are doing business with corporates.

There are some key questions to think about and then record in as much detail as you need. We will talk about some of those details later, in the Mindset chapter. For now, you choose whether the detail in your answer is 1 word, 1000 words or an interpretive dance.

If it is interpretive dance, please record it and send it to me. I would love to see that. I imagine it as a flowing classical ballet style, but it is yours, so you do what you want.

First question is, who you want to work with. I suggest that you write a list of ideal clients. Dream as big as you like. If you sell products, you may want to think of who your ideal buyers are and also who are your ideal customers.

Not only where do you want to see your product stocked but who do want to see using it? Is it someone famous or a group of people? Go wild here and record everyone you would like to have as a client. I am not going to advise you to try to secure them all at once. I will take you through how to choose who to start to target. That is tactics and for now, we are in strategy. If an ideal client comes to mind, you are not going to edit them out by thinking they are too big for me or that won't happen. Write them down. No one client is too big for you to aim for. You are done with playing or feeling small.

If you are used to doing that type of strategic work, feel free to use whatever works for you. I love lists and mind mapping.

If this is new, then here are some approaches that you could try.

Mind map – get a sheet of A3 paper and write future clients in the centre and draw a circle around that. Now start to draw lines coming away from the circle and add in the names of your future clients. You can do it by industry, individual, by country or as random as you like.

If you already have some corporate clients or leads, then also add them in here and make it clear they are existing by either colour coding, adding the word 'existing', or have them on a separate branch.

I got into mind mapping after attending a conference where Tony Buzan was the main speaker. I'm pretty much an auditory learner, which makes me a words person. I do have a secondary preference of visual in my learning style, but I hadn't really got into mind mapping at the time. It was all the rage as Tony had written his book and it had become a best-seller. I worked in the education sector at the time, and it was becoming very popular.

I went along to the conference and it was, to this day, one of the best I have ever attended. Tony's explanation of how mind mapping works neurologically was fascinating. I have used it ever since. I'm a professional problem solver and the answer to every big strategic problem starts on a large sheet of A3 for me.

It progresses from there into a structure, but it all begins in the mind map when I am sifting and sorting ideas, creating or building a strategy. I am still an auditory learner and one of the ways we auditory learners work though ideas is that we talk them through.

If that isn't you, it might explain why you know some people who start to talk though an idea, explore it out loud and then reach a different conclusion at the end of the discussion. It is because that is a learning style that works for them. It is partly why those of use who deliver training break people into pairs and groups to talk. It isn't so we can have a rest. It is because the auditory folk learn well that way. The other reason is, of course, the sharing of knowledge and experience, that shared cognitive diversity which is lifeblood in adult learning.

I will let you into a little secret if you don't tell anyone? Promise? Ok, well, when I am doing the mind mapping, I am not visual enough to only do that. So, I have a little chat with myself as I do it. Nothing too in depth, just a little mutter through the ideas. It helps me get it all down. I invite you to do this too if it helps. Just be aware that if you occasionally do it in an open office, people may notice.

This is a habit I had even in corporate and my amazing friend Tamarra once said to me 'I love how you have a chat with yourself sometimes'. Ooops!

If you are a visual learner, then mind mapping with the accompanying self chatter as an option might be fine. If you are a kinesthetic learner, you might work best in motion, so the physical act of writing the mind map will help. You can also consider doing it on a white board or whilst walking, although the model nature of a mind map often appeals to the kinesthetics among you anyway.

If you have that list, then we will move on to the next question

What do you want your working life to look like?

Work a month and earn a million? This is the wrong book for you then. I can recommend some amazing specialists on passive income or property or investing, but working with corporates in the beginning will not be a make-money-whilst-you-sleep type of scenario.

I should add that the people I know who work a few hours and earn huge sums did not start out that way. They worked incredibly hard to become overnight successes!

You are going to have to put some hours into making this plan, putting it into practice and then doing the actual work that you win with corporates. So, the reason you need to ask yourself 'what do I want my working life to look like?' is so that right now, you can create a vision of what that looks like and then you, with my help, will build a future that looks like that.

When you start winning repeat corporate work, you can end up busy. During the first covid outbreak in 2020, I won so much work at one point that I worked 12-hour days, 7 days a week, for a period of time.

It wasn't too much of a problem because I was used to that from my corporate roles and the world was effectively closed, so having a major distraction was a good escape. It also meant that for me, the first lock down flew past, but I wouldn't have been able to do it for a prolonged period. It also means that I really appreciated having a supportive husband who did what he could to make that easier and never once complained about being left on his own to get through a pandemic.

I made a conscious choice at that time to sign all the contracts I had won because:

- I believed it was unlikely the lockdown, which had just been announced, would only be two weeks

- I have worked like that before when I was in corporate jobs in a salaried role
- All of the work was interesting work that I had very high motivation to do
- It was all with my dream clients
- I knew the end date, therefore how long I would have to be able to work that way
- I was able to bring others I trusted quickly into my business to help deliver
- I knew when I started my business what I wanted my working life to look like. It had not been 12 hours x 7, but a pandemic was a game-changer and I had to make an immediate adjustment

What I want you to think about now is this: What does your ideal working life look like?

Not a small change or even a steep change from what you have now, but your ideal state in your working life. Write down what comes to mind.

Here are some prompts to help you:

How much are you working? Do you do that in hours per day, week or year?

My ideal when I started my business was 8 hours per day, 4 days per week, over a 40-week year. I didn't mind if that averaged out in an inconsistent way. I still work a bit more than that now because I am building an additional business to give myself some passive income and grow wealth, but I am close to moving to that ideal.

When the pandemic hit, I had been in business long enough to know that one of the aspects I loved about my working life was the variety. Working with multiple clients in different fields was raising my game. It was allowing me to pick up parts of best practice and share it with or deliver it to other clients. I was learning and growing and therefore my offer to my clients was improving.

I was also enjoying the variety of people that I could choose to work with. I knew I wanted those things to remain as part of my working life. Therefore, if I could make enough to build a bit of a financial buffer then, if some fallow times did come, I could ride them out instead of having to go back to a job.

I am going to be very clear - I am not anti job or anti being an employee. I might one day have a job again. I'm not looking at that right now but I have a never say never approach because who knows, one day, they might discover that tall middle-aged women make great jockeys, and that dream will be revived. I just didn't want to have to get a job then, so a short-term choice to mitigate the risk of derailing my longer-term plans was a calculated and planned risk.

I want you to be as conscious about these decisions now so that as you start to see corporate work coming in, you can make those choices consciously too.

Thinking about how much you want to work will also help you with pricing, which is one of the aspects of corporate work that I hear entrepreneurs struggle with. I will take you through some help with pricing in later chapters.

What percentage of your business do you want to be corporate work? The only right answer here is one that works for you.

When I started my business, I only wanted to do corporate work, so it was 100% of my working time that was my goal.

If you have a business-to-consumer market right now, you must think about how much of that you want to keep. If it consumes you every waking or working minute, how much of that are you going to reduce in the short term or long term?

If you are screaming out that you cannot reduce that at all, and it is all your time, then I am going to be your critical friend that pushes you gently at this point. If you are so busy that you cannot make any time free, then we must pause and go back to chapter 3 - Confirm your Why.

We had that chat about why now and how if you can't do it now, you need to build in the time to do it and start then. This book and this method will help you do this efficiently and effectively. It will save you wasting time on chasing wild geese and get you hyper focused on work that you want to do and can win. It will not generate more hours in the day for you.

Right now, you want to decide how much time in your working week can you dedicate to doing this work. Pop it right in the diary, make a recurring appointment to develop working with corporates. If it is an hour, then that is an hour more than you had in your diary last week.

Now what about long term? Do you want to have all your time working with corporates? Half of it? Again, this is about finding the right answer with you. A lot of people love having a business-to-business and a business-to-consumer part of their business. Do not let anyone tell you that you should only focus on the highest paid work.

You didn't start your own business to let other people's narratives run your business. If you only want to do the highest paid work, then you go ahead if it is your choice or even if it is your necessity. We all have those bills to pay.

If you want to do a mix because that is what lights your fire, then have that as part of your vision.

The great thing about this vision is this is your starting vision. Every year you can revisit it and redefine what you want, if you want.

How much do you need to earn from corporate work?

How much do you want to earn? Ok, I admit that is a bit of a trick question. Really there are two questions here. How much do you need to earn? Then how much do you want to earn?

Here is how to work this out:

How much does your business need to operate? In the corporate world, this is talked about as OPEX. That stands for Operating Expenditure.

Now, whether you are a sole trader and drawing a salary or a director and taking dividends, how much do you need to be paid? If you don't know that then I recommend you spend some time on understanding that

Tip: if you are reading this thinking that:

- you do not really like to look at numbers in that way;
- that you are not really a number person; or
- that you run a business, but you spend what is there

with no deeper thought or look at what it costs you then I beseech you to pause.

If you start to enter the corporate world and you cannot financially navigate your own business, then you are in grave danger of working very hard to not make any money. That is no one's vision.

If it is your reality, then I suspect that you might have money mindset issues going on. If you have a whole load of stories in your head about how or why you can be a business owner who does not bother to look at the finances, then my critical friend voice has returned to tell you that you owe this to yourself.

You do not need to become a financial, economics or accounting whizz kid. You do need to know how much it costs you to run your business. You also want to explore why you are not doing that.

I'm not talking about doing your own accounts here. I am talking about understanding at what point of income you have paid the bills and are now starting to make a profit. If you don't know what it costs you, you are going to hit a major barrier when it comes to pricing.

In the meantime, trust me that you need to work this out and let's do the work.

So, list all the costs involved in operating your business:

Consider:

- Wages
- Materials

- Premises
- Taxes
- Etc.

What about a pension contribution? Have you included that in the above items, or do you want to make it a separate line now? If you don't want to work until you expire, you should be including this in your need to earn. Your financial future isn't an 'extra', it is an essential. You can be flexible in your first couple of years in business as you build your business. Longer term, realistically to replace a job, which comes with pension contributions, then you should be including pension contributions for yourself.

So, now you know what you need for your business to run.

Now how about what you would like your business to make?

How to think of that? Well, you could dream and come up with a big number. Perfectly acceptable. If you want to make £1k per month, £10k per month, £100k per month... whatever. You do you here and write it down. You will have to work out how you will do it, but we will get to that.

Another way is to work out what you like to make based on this:

- What you need to operate (OPEX)
- What you need to pay yourself
- What you need to pay in tax

Think about what you want to spend on projects, buying new goods or systems. This is called capital expenditure and is referred to as CAPEX in the corporate world. It is treated differently for tax purposes and there are rules around what is OPEX and what is CAPEX. CAPEX is treated as you investing in your business or your business assets and is treated differently for that reason, so it is important that you check with your tax authority or your accountant when treating certain costs as CAPEX.

Once you have written down all those numbers, write down what you want them to be in future.

So now you have where you are now and what you want your future income to be.

When I first started my business, it looked like this:

OPEX = 5k 1st year

CAPEX= 4k 1ST year

I knew by year 3 if I couldn't pay my OPEX costs, plus a salary of £130k and a pension contribution of £40k, then I should go back to working in a corporate role. That wouldn't have been an enormous hardship to me as I had thrived in most of my corporate jobs, had a great network and loved the work challenges and the corporate environment.

However, about halfway through my first year something began to shift in me. You see, I enjoyed the freedom I was experiencing even more. Was I working much less? Not really but everything I was doing was totally focused on my goals. I was implementing my own business plans and strategy. I was deploying the tactical elements of creating a pipeline of work. I was starting to collaborate with other people and companies that I was drawn to. I was doing corporate work for clients that focused on the outputs and outcomes for them.

You see, when you have a senior corporate role you have the day job, the leadership role, your personal and professional development and then all the extra 'opportunities' that come your way. When you work in a big corporate, an 'opportunity' is code for a large piece of extra work that may or may not raise your profile, expand your experience, expertise or network.

It also must be added to the existing workload and you will be expected to deliver it on top of your existing workload and objectives with a smile. Don't get me wrong, some of the opportunities that I got in corporate were fantastic. Really interesting pieces of work to get my teeth into. Things that I felt privileged to be asked to lead or to do. All of them were at the cost of my own personal time. I don't regret any of that or grudge any of that time as it made a great career and set an amazing foundation for me to start my own business.

What I had realised though in year 1 is that those 'opportunities' in your own business are the ones you choose or put yourself forward for. And that was a game-changer for me.

Around the start of year 2, a great corporate role came up. It was in my hometown, my business niche, doing what I loved, a 6-figure salary with great terms and conditions, with people I knew I would love working with. I was asked about applying and I had to give it some thought. Ultimately though, I knew that I was loving my new way of working in corporate. Core hours that I sold as consulting were at the call of the client. All other hours I spent on the business, on business development were all about my own opportunities and I wasn't ready to change that. There were two other factors at play too. My business plan had me forecast that by year 3, I needed to be able to replace that corporate salary plus pension or get a job. The same time the job came up, I knew financially I was on track to make double what I wanted in year 3 but make it in year 2.

Finally, my son had joined my business due to covid pausing his career as a chef. It wasn't clear then how long that would last, so I wasn't keen to push him back into that world when it was so volatile.

What was the clearest to me though was how I wanted my life to be. I was enjoying being much more the mistress of my own destiny.

So, I share this with you so that now you have considered the financials you can start to ask yourself the Life Questions.

How do you want to feel about each of these areas?

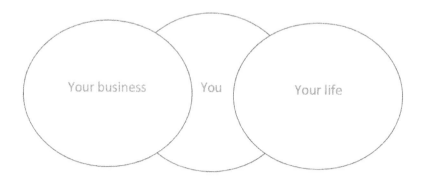

It is important to consider this in a lot of detail because the separation between each of those is less distinct for business owners than for those in employment.

- What do each of those feel like now?

- What will be different when you make the change?
- How do you feel differently?
- How will you dress?
- Where will you go on holiday?
- What will your office or work space look and feel like?
- Do you have a team?
- What does your team look like?
- What do you spend your money on?
- How do you spend your time?

Now put those together into the outline vision. Think of it and write in the present tense but as if you are already the future you. Write about that future that is yours and it will help you make it happen. Not because you are going to magically manifest it (if you do, well done to you) but because you are already telling your brain that it is real. Convince yourself that is your future and you have taken a massive step toward making it happen.

You have done the thinking already in this chapter so now we are pulling it together.

Write this out with your vision in the blanks.

I run a business selling [fill in the blank with your offering] to [fill in as many clients as you plan to have]. My turnover is [fill in your income] and I make a profit of [fill in your profit]. I work [fill in how many hours you work either per week or month] working [fill in how many weeks you work per year].

I feel [fill in how you feel about you] and what I love most about my business is [fill in what you love most]

I have a life of what and I spend time with who doing what. The thing I most love about it is _____ and _____.

Now you have that vision, we will work on the finer details of making it happen. You might come back and make some adjustments once we do.

5

RESEARCH YOUR IDEAL CLIENTS OR INDUSTRY

N ow that you know what you are going to gain and how amazing your life is going to be when you start getting corporate work, we will start to look deeper into how to make that happen.

Research is your key to getting your first corporate contract and to developing and maintaining a pipeline. Research is going to be part of your business from now on. You are about to become a research fiend and it is going to make you more successful than you already are. You will do research every single day from now until you stop your business. I would like you not to panic at this point as I am going to teach you a mix of strategies that are going to have you being such a good researcher that you actually do it in your sleep.

You can be sleeping or swanning around the world and the research will be rolling in to feed your research fiend desires.

And if you really hate research, I'll give some advice on how to outsource it.

Firstly, your research structure. You need to know what you are researching and why. Then you need a research plan, some research tools and an annual review cycle.

So why are you bothering? Why don't I tell you where you need to go to find out what you need to know about who you want to sell to?

Well quite simply, it depends. It changes, and it always will.

We start with keeping it simple. From chapters 3 and 4, you now know who you want to work with and why.

What you need next is to understand as much about them as you can before you begin to shape offers for them and approach them to do business together. Maybe you have already made some corporate sales and you think you could skip this part and keep on doing what you are doing. You could do that, but do you know how you are making those sales? Do you know how to consistently repeat those sales? Would you like it all to seem a bit easier? Then stick with this chapter.

Why would anyone writing a book counsel you not to skip a chapter? Well, my entrepreneur friend, I know that you are an expert at figuring out what to choose to fill your time with. You spend every day having to make choices between the million things that need to be done and choose which one to go at. A little chapter skip here and there can't harm anyone, can it? I also know that not everyone loves the research.

I am a research fiend by nature and by training. If I want to work with a new client, I will read everything I can find, attend whichever events I can legally access and enjoy becoming so entrenched in the research that if they were an individual, they would issue a restraining order.

I must make sure that my annual strategy and plan for the pipeline does not permit me to spend 40 hours per week only researching.

I digress. How do I know that some business owners do not like to do the research? Simple. I have seen it glaring out at me from their bids for corporate work. I have seen it both on a small and large scale. On several occasions, it has been the deciding factor between them not getting the work.

It does not matter if you have the most sophisticated of graphics, beautifully structured paperwork, enticing proposals describing your offer. If you make it clear that you have not spent any time on figuring out what my problems and objectives are, or worse, what the actual business we conduct is, you will not progress very far in a procurement process.

There is so much information readily available on companies that there is not much forgiveness for companies who do not do some basic research and make it clear that they did the homework. These people assessing you may be planning to spend a lot of money with you. They want to have their confidence raised with each interaction. Doing good research - and showing it - is a highly valuable way to do that.

I do think that the amount of information is one of the stumbling blocks that entrepreneurs can trip over. With so much to do, where do you start? What is useful? And what is proportionate?

First, let's talk about how much you can do at any one time.

If you have decided to work with corporates and have no experience whatsoever in that area, I suggest you make one of two choices to start. Choose either a maximum of two companies or one industry to start with.

Once you have gone through this systematic approach to research on these, you can begin to replicate it repeatedly and maintain it in an efficient way. However, if you start trying to research multiple industries and companies, you will either spread yourself so thin that the research will be superficial or not from good sources. If you wonder what I mean by that, I can tell you that whilst Google and Wikipedia are great resources, they are not always great sources.

The other alternative is that you do it all, but you are exhausted, bored or down a research rabbit hole so deep that your business is wondering where you have gone to.

Once you have chosen your two companies or your one industry, there are some next steps that will essentially lead you down the same research path.

If you are going with an industry, you are going to look at who are the four or five key players in that industry. Which of those would you most like to work with? Whittle it down to two.

Either way, we now have a maximum of two companies.

Whichever industry you are going to focus on, it will have some trade press. Every industry has a trade press. Some of it is free. Get subscribed to that. Some of it is paid. You can often get access to these as online copies through your local library. Or you can pay for a subscription. It may not be the most scintillating read but it is using the language and imagery that your clients expect. You will gain so much insight from this. You will see who is already working with them, what events they attend, who are the big names, what are the big trends. It may not be thrilling but it is a gold mine of knowledge.

Next are company web pages. Not the top of the page but scroll down, right down to the bottom where only you, me and the journalists are mining for that gold. The least read page is often 'about us'. For you, this is another source of valuable information. It will tell you things you should now such as:

How is the company structured?

Who are they?

Some organisations will have a high-level organisation chart that tells you how the company is divided up into divisions, departments, directorates or functions. These all pretty much mean the same thing. The reason that they are important to you is that you want to know which part of the company you are selling into. That is different from who is buying.

Any large company will have a procurement team or a set of buyers. These are people whose job it is to buy what is needed for the company in the right volume, at the right price and at the right time. They will have items and services they buy for themselves but mostly, they are buying on behalf of the departments who need the goods, services or works. Remember I said a large company is like a small town? Well think of the procurement team as being like the shoppers for that town.

We will look at how you get to know a procurement team and get on their lists later but for now, your early research will give you some insights into who might need what you offer.

If there are named individuals, record those names in your research records. Now here is how you start to make the research happen in your sleep. Remember those key individuals you found in the 'about us' section or the company blogs or newsletters? The ones that you saw and thought 'they need what I offer'? You are going to do two things with those names. First one is to look them up on LinkedIn. If it is a big company, you may only be able to follow them, not connect with them.

If they are following only then follow them. If you can connect with them, then do that. There are lots of specialists on LinkedIn and I do read them. Some say don't send any messages, just send a request. Others say write a personal message. Others say keep a simple message such as 'Hi, I am trying to grow my network and would like to connect with you'.

My advice is you do you. Figure out which of those works for you, find a LinkedIn guru and follow them if you don't already. I'm a bit fickle with LinkedIn gurus. There is one I know is good but too shouty for me. I look at some who operate in different countries, as the cultural differences in the workplace mean that I take a different approach where appropriate.

My approach to accepting requests is I say yes to everyone. If they do anything weird, I block them. To be honest, I get a lot less weird stuff on LinkedIn than any other social media, so I happily accept.

I rarely get round to replying to direct messages from strangers just trying to sell to me. The reason is simple - whatever I need to buy, I go to my network.

We will come back to how you will use that information shortly. For now, back to the research.

What are their values? How do they align with what you thought they were? What about your values and what you know of their reputation?

What are their objectives?

You want to know what the company is trying to achieve this year, next year and any future years. As you read through these statements, look for the ways that you know that what you offer would help them meet that need. Write it down as you can make direct reference to this correlation and it is highly powerful.

You might think of it as corporate bumf. It is likely in someone's objectives and they are sitting figuring out how to meet that objective. If you pop up as part of the solution, that is massively helpful.

Annual accounts

If the company publishes annual accounts, there are four really important things you want to ascertain form these:

How viable are they? (You want to be paid, don't you?)

How much did they spend on what you offer? If it is zero, make sure you know why you want to start getting them to buy it and how you will align that with their objectives. A change in the law can be a good example here.

How much do they plan to spend next year on what you offer?

What are their biggest challenges? Again, focus on how you help with those.

Annual accounts may not be the biggest page turner but they give you a lot of information about a large company. They will mention any significant challenges, maybe in there is something you can connect your product or services to helping them solve.

Other sources

You might be able to find something called a Business Scorecard. Not everywhere has one but if they do, it is useful for you as you can see where they are focusing their attention and thus, their spending.

Look for things like board meetings, AGM minutes that are published or public. You will be surprised at the number of companies that publish their Annual General meeting minutes. There are also a number that publish their board minutes. Some of them will be redacted, which is a posh way of saying some stuff is blacked out. There are good reasons for this, usually around confidentiality.

Who is reading these, you may ask? Journalists often do. And me. After years sitting in these types of meetings, I know that there can be gold in those minutes, sometimes it is explicit and sometimes you must read between the lines.

I remember when I worked in corporate, I was headhunted for another role. It was an industry I knew well but a company I did not know well. I read about a years' worth of their board minutes (I am more fun at parties than I am making this sound).

I spotted a theme around transparency coming up again and again. When I went for the interview, I asked about the reason for this. Turned out there had been a bit of a rocky road and the previous chief executive had left because there was a perception that the company wasn't being transparent enough and was bending with political will too easily. Given that the role they were interviewing me for was strategic and involved managing stakeholders, including political stakeholders, they were impressed that I had done my homework in that depth and could spot the covert references to the problem.

If I was a firm who helps organisations manage their data or with their strategic communication or marketing, that information is useful. I can add it into a pitch to show that I know that they are on a journey to be more transparent and that it is important that they are also seen to be transparent in the public eye... and then I would show how I can help them with that.

Pouring over those documents might not seem a great Friday night but when you find a little nugget that gives you insight, it is worth it. Maybe a Tuesday morning makes it more palatable.

In my first year in my own consulting business, I was working with a large company who had a major infrastructure project to deliver. Part of my research was to read all the public documents about the board running the project. It was high profile, so many people across different organisations in this one city made up the board. I was to coach and mentor the project lead. I knew that the technical side of the project was complex but nothing that I had to really investigate. I knew that the profile of the project politically was where the real challenges would lie. So, I looked up the website. Strange, no board minutes published in 18 months. I took a note and added it to my research file for that client.

When I started coaching the client, I mentioned it. The client wasn't aware of the fact that the board hadn't met or published any minutes. He knew right away that for him, as the project leader, this meant his key stakeholders were not sitting down collectively to look at progress reports, discuss any challenges or views that they had. He also knew that there was a big change coming in his projects and that the board minutes would be scrutinised by the media, trade press and local elected officials.

He took immediate action. He called each board member to check in with them. Got an understanding of why they hadn't been meeting and got a virtual meeting arranged as a conference call. This was pre covid, so the lack of time had been a major factor in the board not meeting. He also got them to add to the end of each set of minutes that the board only meets by exception and no longer on a quarterly basis.

It is a minor example, but a little research can help you be informed and helpful. It established that I do enough research on my clients to be perceptive.

The more research you can do, the better placed you are to communicate well with your client. You will also be more able to align what you offer with what they need. Your brain will start to make the connections

So, get curious... and then get more curious. I'm talking close to obsessed level if you have the time. The more you absorb, the better. Make sure you have the useful information stored somewhere.

Once you have completed the research on your first one, you repeat the process for everyone else you want to work with.

Eventually, you will have built up a bank of research and knowledge on various potential clients. If your end goal is to have a pipeline of work flowing in, this is a crucial asset. When we come to Chapter 10 - Take it to Market, I will explain more about your pipeline and how you are going to set it up.

I have recently hired a research assistant to spend 3 hours per week doing this for my business. Part of her role is to research potential clients and gather specific targeted information that I need to bring new clients into my pipeline. The other role is researching for projects which we are working on for clients. I still need to read the output from the research, but I can save a lot of time by having someone who is hyper focused on this and knows the industries we work in and knows how to carry out effective research.

In the beginning though, before I could commit to funding a post to do research, I would spend about 8 hours per week on research. I would set aside some time each day to read key information. I would often use any breaks that I had to look whilst grabbing something to eat or drink. Hey, don't judge me, I am not saying that is good for your health, but I promised not to

76

pretend I did all this in a normal working week. I also love to read; it is my favorite medium for learning. So, if you love to watch videos you can probably save yourself time by doing that. Me, well I am probably going to read the transcript.

Getting it organised

Firstly, set up a folder with your potential client's name that you want to work with in your email inbox. The reason for this is so that your everyday email inbox isn't flooded with research. This makes it distracting and means you end up glancing at it and then filing it for later. Later, for busy entrepreneurs, translates to never. You know that time when you have nothing else to do but catch up on all the deferred things? Exactly. It doesn't exist.

Now you are going to put some time in your diary to review the folder. I suggest for your first one 30 minutes per week. As you get more and more used to doing this, you will need less time per client as you get accustomed to seeing what you need to know and what is dross or not relevant.

Likewise, as you start to work with clients and your pipeline is pumping away bringing you in regular work from existing and new clients, you will know what you need to keep an eye open for and when you need to delve into details.

Now you need some juicy information flowing into that inbox.

There are some hacks that will save you time and I will share them with you here. For each of these, you want to set an automatic rule in your email inbox that these emails will go straight into the folder in the name of your client that you have just set up.

If the client you want to work with has an option to sign up for either updates or newsletters, sign up to them. Have those go straight into the folder too.

Free research tools

Set up a Google news alerts with the name of your client and any sub names, group names or trading names they go by. This means every time a piece of news is published that Google could find, it will pop into that folder (you did set up that email rule, didn't you?) waiting on when you have time to read it.

If your target client is a brand that is led by the person who runs it, you might want to put their name on a Google alert into that folder too. If you want to work with a more traditional or conservative corporate, that might not be as relevant as they are likely to have CEOs who keep a lower profile and are always referred to as 'First Name, Second Name of Large Corporate', thus the google alert will pick that up anyway. When you have personality led brands, they might be quoted in the media without their brand being named.

Create a folder for each client or industry and store all of the information in there until you need it.

Industry events

Now your dream day might not be wandering around an exhibition space at the international Festival of Work, The Farm Business Show Exhibition or the International Food and Drink event, but let me reframe that for you. Would you like to wander around an enormous space, filled with people who want to look at, discuss, explore and buy what you offer? If that's not a 'hell yeah' then I don't know what is. Many of these events are also free. They make most of their money from people who book the stands and sponsor the shows. The sponsorship is a great clue to what types of companies will be there.

Sign up to all the events that take place in the industries that you want to sell into and yes, you've guessed it, have those emails go into that folder in the emails. You might want at this stage to add one folder for each industry.

Now, as those emails start to come in, you can have a look at the events and choose which ones are likely to be best for you to attend. We are all grown up here so it is up to you how you choose which ones. Maybe you only go to free ones, or ones nearby or ones with a certain footfall or sponsor.

Over time, you can evolve to looking at those emails and going onto the event website to look for opportunities for you to pitch yourself as a speaker or workshop host. This is a great way to get yourself out there, talking to multiple people at once. If that feels too uncomfortable now, don't worry, you can work on that over time. Confidence is a journey, not a goal. For now, it is fine to start by signing up, attending and wandering around talking to people, building your network and growing that confidence.

If there are seminars or workshops, think about the ones your likely clients will attend, not the ones you fancy the most, and sign up to those. Chat to people and ask questions, not master-mind quick fire style but about their roles and their work. Start to understand more about their world and think about how what you offer matches up to their needs.

If you are already on solid ground on what your offer to them would be, then you can start to talk to people about that. These are potential clients, and they are in shopping mode! In the sales terminology, you can't get a hotter lead.

Also, be aware some folk might only be having a day out of the office, so chill it if they don't want to talk shop with you.

Outsource advice

If you are going to outsource the research on your potential clients, you have two options.

You can go to a company whose sole business is to research clients. Based on what you tell them, they will either send you leads of bids that companies have put out there that you can try to win, or put you in contact with those companies. They will either charge you for their time, at a set package or on commission. I have never had to work with any of them as, by using my own methodology, my pipeline keeps bringing me the work. If you are going down that route, make sure you check who else they have worked with. See if you can speak to existing clients and see what type of work they are winning and how good the return on their investment is. Also, make sure you know how long the commitment to working with them is so that if it doesn't work for you, you know when you can exit the commitment.

Your other option is to hire someone into your team or a freelancer to do the research. You write up a specific research brief based on what you need to know, give them the companies or industry and a list of what you want to know including the above and also things such as what are they buying? How much of it and at what price?

When my business was growing so much that I couldn't do all the research, read it, develop the pipeline and do the work, I brought in a research assistant. She was at university, studying in a field that many of my clients work in. Due to being at university, she was researching regularly anyway so she knew how to navigate and find good sources to feed me reliable and detailed research about my prospective clients.

A little tip here is that a new prospective client may also do a little research on you. Have a look at what they are going to find and make sure you are making the right digital first impression. Here is how I would look for you if you had approached me when I worked in corporate, if I was thinking of bringing you in:

- Your LinkedIn profile page
- Your LinkedIn business page
- Website
- Companies house search
- Google News search
- Facebook search

Do them now and tidy up anything that needs it.

6

PROPOSAL DEFINITION

Your proposal is your offer to corporates. Now that you know why, who you want to sell to, how much you want to make from that and you have the research on who is buying it or who will want to buy it, you must start to bring that together.

Looking at that research that you have done, you need to check off some points.

Is your proposed client already buying what you sell? If they are, then you know that there is a demand for that. Now you also know that they have a supplier.

So, you have choices. Why should they buy from you instead of their existing supplier?

Are you going to be cheaper, better, different, the same? Do you have a new way of doing the work or is your product better at achieving the outcomes they want?

Really think about what your competitor offers and what is different for a client to use you? Perhaps your competitor is struggling to meet the demand? Or you know your client will buy double next year so you want to be an additional supplier.

You also have the option of approaching the existing supplier. Could you collaborate with them? Or be a subcontractor, subconsultant or supplier to them? Some of my best work has come from working in collaboration with companies that traditionally would be my competitors. However, those that would be competitors where I valued their work, admired their values and knew that they worked with my ideal clients, I approached and told them that I would like to work with them.

Really, what you are trying to work out here is your silver bullet, your unique selling point specific to the client you want. If you have a product, what is so special about that? Is it the product itself or is it how you source the raw materials or how you manufacture it? Perhaps your product has a higher quality, lower carbon footprint or higher profit margin? Maybe it is all three!

It can even be that you are new. New is the most powerful word in marketing. Why do you think laundry detergent companies are bringing out new products all the time? Is it because they are worried that we all stop washing our clothes? That suddenly no one decides to wear clean clothes again? Nope. It is because they are constantly trying to have a competitive advantage over other brands.

They can do that in two ways, marketing and pricing. They know that the word new is the number one attraction in marketing. I have worked in change management and projects for decades now and I often think it is funny how many people don't like change, but they respond to the word new?

So, they bring out a new flavour. Well, they bring out a new scent, but you know what I mean. And guess what? It works.

Just like these mega companies, part of your proposal can be that you are new. You have a new product or a new service or that you are newly offering it. If you are really struggling to differentiate yourself from the rest of the supply and competition, then starting with being new is a good place.

I mentioned that soap powder companies have two strategies to compete. Marketing and pricing. Well, pricing is the second part of defining your proposal that we need to look at.

This is different for services and products, so I have written them up separately here for ease.

Services

Worried that you have no idea what to charge corporates? If you have been selling to consumers or have just started in business, this can be a tricky one.

Here are some of the statements I hear:

- I think I should charge corporates more but don't want to price myself out of winning the work
- I don't want to go too low first time getting corporate work and then not be able to raise my prices
- I don't know what everyone else is charging

- I'm not sure whether I should charge more or less than my competitors
- I don't know what my competitors are charging
- I don't know who to ask for advice
- I hear some of the day rates being paid and think no one would pay that for me.

Here is the thing that you need to know. Every intelligent client in a big corporate wants their supplier to make a profit.

Yes, it is true.

They want you to make a profit.

You know why? Because suppliers who don't make money go to the wall. They go under, they go bust. The best case is that they disappear into the ether, never to be heard of again.

Worst case is that they go under whilst they are working for you. First the quality drops. This is 100% guaranteed as no one is running their business at a peak performance level whilst facing bankruptcy. Next, they disappear mid contract. They are no longer allowed to trade which means you cannot have their service. Even though you are still in contract with them.

Now this can be a huge problem or a minor problem. Whatever the scale, it is a problem. You see, in corporate you are still trying to deliver your objectives, meet your targets, deliver you scorecard and now, you have no supplier for at least one part of that.

Whether that person is training your team, building your project or something else, you now have no one to take that forward. Sometimes they may even hold materials or resources that you need. Guess what? They now belong to the liquidator and you can't access them very easily.

The final straw is that the corporate organisation now must go back out to the market and start the procurement process all over again to replace that supplier.

A right old pain it is.

This is why sensible corporate clients want you to make money.

They also want to buy your services at a rate that is completive and within their budget.

So, we need to work out what you are going to charge.

You may eventually have several rates that vary by work, by client, by industry, by country, but we will start with the basics.

What you charge corporates is likely to be higher than what you charge selling direct to consumers. There are a few reasons why it is perfectly acceptable to charge corporates more.

Firstly, there is the fact that you may have higher overheads. You are likely to have costs that you may not need for selling to consumers. This could include areas such as meeting quality standards and or getting certified for quality accreditations.

You may also have to be a member of a professional institute or perhaps several. You may have to pay fees to belong to a trade association. Don't panic that you must join these now, but they are memberships you will want to have when you are growing or maintaining a pipeline of work, so do account for them in your current pricing.

You will need insurance to cover your working with corporates too. As a minimum, you will need whatever level of professional indemnity is common in your industry. I also have insurance for all my tech, employee liability and key person cover. If you have employees, you are legally obliged to have employee liability insurance. You may want to look at what you will need and work out the costs. If you hadn't already included this, go back and add it to your OPEX costs.

Another one you should consider is if you must travel overseas for the work, then this is not often covered in the standard holiday insurance that you will have, so take a separate policy or add it on.

Supply and demand

Then there is the good old law of supply and demand. Personally, I knew that I was super niche in the role I played in projects and had experience of being a professional head of that discipline in two continents. I knew that I had a massive network in the major projects and rail world, and that there weren't many people with that experience. I knew that supply was short for what I could offer, therefore, I wanted to offer a boutique consultancy service in my niche with pricing to reflect that.

Now, I had to have a back up plan as demand for niches can be lower, so whilst the pricing is higher, that reflects the fact that the demand may be lower and hey, I had those bills to pay too!

So, my back up was a lower rate for more generic work. I had a list of various places that I could go to if I needed to generate some income at a lower rate but higher volume. I haven't had to do any of that but contingency planning for risk is as much about letting your brain and your gut know that you have a plan, or some recourse if the risk transpires.

You want to make sure you have covered doing some research into how much supply there is and what the demand levels are in your industry or in the service area you want to sell to corporates.

Competitor pricing

You can also make it simple and look at what your competitors are charging and charge around that price. You can offer a marginally lower rate in your first year if you need to bring in some income and you want to have a slight competitive advantage. Although new is a great marketing word, you may want to do a very minor reduction until corporates clients get used to seeing the value of your work and results you deliver.

Price hikes

It is fine to raise your prices in line with inflation, RPI or whatever you choose as your annual uplift. I chose not to raise my prices in a year that one of my main industries saw public sector pay freezes, mass redundancies and funding cuts. For me, it was a values-led decision that it didn't seem palatable to me to put my prices up at that time. What I did do was tell my clients that and be clear that it was a conscious decision.

Discounts

Discounts can be tempting to offer when you need to generate income. However, be very careful as it can be hard to get back to full price. It does depend on how you feel and how well you know your market and how much you want to land a particular client. If you know that they are the gateway to a whole industry or to other clients, you can consider it. It is not something to rush into though and if you work with a coach or mentor, then it is worth talking through with them.

I will share with you my approach and hopefully that helps you. Hey, let's face it, you are too darn good and valuable to be discounting yourself. Discount to get discounted at times.

I can tell you that I have looked at some low bids for corporate work over the years and everyone in the room has asked what is wrong with them. What have they missed out etc.?

For anyone selling services to corporates, I would recommend you only offer a discount for bulk and that also must be guaranteed work. For anything below two full days per week for six months, I don't offer any reduction in my day rate.

For anything over that, it is by agreement only and only on certain types of work.

For training courses, I may offer a free place for a certain number of places bought.

Do I lose out on some work because I don't discount heavily enough? Yes. I have point blank said 'I am sorry, I do not work at that day rate, but I can recommend someone else who does and is excellent'.

I have never once regretted those decisions.

By year 2 in my business, I realised that I could offer value to clients with work at different days rates for work that I could oversee, but bring in freelancers to deliver. This worked well because I only worked with freelancers whom I knew and trusted. Self starters who crack on with the work and deliver a ton of value to my clients. I don't make a high amount of money on this activity but I do make a reasonable amount, it has improved the outcomes and quality of work on several contracts and of course, it offers a solution that clients ask for.

Consultants

If you are planning to do consulting work, you can approach whoever you want to freelance for and if they are interested in working with you, they will be able to tell you how much they would pay you as a day rate.

Remember that they will be putting a mark up on that to any clients that they sell you to. I get asked a lot how much this and the real answer is, it depends. Some charge a percentage; others add a rate per day. Some might even not add anything as they want to impress the clients by providing you. You can end up being used as a loss leader if you are someone they know offers real value to a client.

I spent many years assessing consultants' bids and signing off the bills. I was also about to sell into the industry that I had come from for the most part, so I knew the range of day rates for the various levels of consultants.

I combined that with how many days I would have to work to earn the money that I needed, to figure out if my business was viable. If I had to charge way more than the going rate or work more than 220 consulting days per year, I would have known that it was not viable.

There was some work that I wanted to do with other companies that I hadn't worked with before. I didn't really know what the going rate was so I reached out to people in my network and asked them what I could expect to be paid for my services. They were great at offering advice that I could then factor into my pricing.

There is also some work that I decided to do at a lower rate than I would work for anywhere else. There was a very simple reason for that. It was part of my market strategy. You see, it was a company that had a good profile, and working for them would extend my network and would build massive credibility in my industry. They are also a non-profit distribution organisation, with values completely aligned to my own.

They provide adult education and training to people already employed who want to get qualifications, expand their knowledge and improve their career prospects. As someone who left school and didn't get my degree until I was in my thirties, I really value the work they do.

I know how hard it is to start at college level and work right through to post grad level when you are also trying to work full time, raise a family and manage your household. Supporting people going through that process, in an industry I love, goes much deeper for me than money. For that company, I was happy to be able to work at their going rate. It is still a decent rate and I love the value that the work brings to people's lives, so that is a reward beyond money.

I also looked at the information publicly available on various government procurement websites to see what work was being awarded at what value. From that, I could reverse engineer the likely range of costs.

You now need to follow those steps combined with what has come up in your research and see what range of rates you are coming up with. I also run a free Facebook group that you can always come into and ask me and others if your range is about right.

Once you have figured out what you are charging and what you are offering, we need to sense check it.

What does that mean? Well, it means that you make sure that it is all deliverable with why you are doing this, how much you want to earn and how often you want to work. Plus, there are the basic logistics. If you are selling your time a day at a time, the very maximum you can sell is 365 of those days in a year!

There are only 168 hours in any one week and you should spend some of those asleep, some eating, and you may have other activities, such as a life, that you want to account for.

So, if you know that you want to offer out x number of service hours per week or year, whatever works for you, then make sure you look realistically at your planner and see how much time in your life that leaves you.

I'm not going to give you a wordy lecture on how I charge boutique prices and work an hour per week. I do charge

THE GAP IN THE MIDDLE
THE GAP IN THE MIDDLE

boutique prices, but I am also a recovering workaholic. I don't mean a little bit of a workaholic, I mean full on, spending every waking hour working.

I'm also not going to pretend I hated it because I didn't. I bloody loved it. It made me feel successful, motivated and if I admit to ego, a bit important. I know that when I worked some 110-hour weeks, I was secretly (maybe not so secretly) delighted that I had managed to eliminate most of their human needs and deliver really good quality work for every one of those hours.

I was kind of high on the thrill of work at times. I write this partly to get a vicarious thrill out of reliving those days -kind of like when prisoners share tales of the great crimes they committed or addicts revisit blow outs. I can have the thrill of the nostalgia, but only very briefly. Kick me here reader to get me to stop because being a workaholic is like any word ending with -holic. It's bad for you in the end and will reduce the quality of your life or lifespan overall. So, I am not going to lecture you on not working too much and on finding a good work balance. It is great advice, but while I may be a recovering workaholic, I am not a hypocrite. I have had to do some internal work and some business strategy to manage the thrill of getting dopamine hits for working and the highs of working hard or long hours. The best advice I can give you is to figure out your logistics.

If you sell in days, then a reasonable amount of maximum day per year to offer is about 200, maximum.

That accounts for:

- 6 weeks holiday
- 12 days per year working on your business

- 12 days business development
- and 6 days professional / personal development

If you are starting out and have yet to build a whole pipeline of work, you want to allocate more days to business development.

This isn't an exact science, but I find colour coding the days on my electronic diary in outlook and my wall planner at the start of the year means that if I need to change something around, I only consciously cancel or swap around days.

You want to avoid overbooking yourself with clients or giving up all your time for business development, and have a quick way to see that at any time.

If you sell services in batches, such as training or coaching, again you can work it out using the same method. Make sure you also include development, supervision and travel in these, too.

You also want to be very clear that once you know what you plan to sell your offer for, that you also know how you plan to deliver that. We will look at what you will create to demonstrate your proposal to the corporates that you want to work with.

I want to take you through products now and it may be that you actually offer a mix of products and services so stay tuned.

Products are different. If you are already in the product business you already know what your cost per item is to make, retail price and gross and net profit per item. You know those, right?

You are also likely to have looked at where you want to place your product. What? You have more than one? I apologise, and go you! You probably know where your <u>products</u> sit in terms of competitor pricing at retail price.

If you don't, then put this book down. Right now, come on, we are in action taker mode today. Put it down and have a look at who else is selling your products. For the top of the range, who sells 1 per year to a billionaire, to the bargain basement version. Where are you on that continuum? Is it where you want to be?

You have two avenues for getting into corporates. I suspect you also already know which one you want to go for. Either you are set in getting your product into stores or you want to supply to a big corporate who either uses it, does something with or to it and sells it on.

Either way, you are looking to get into a part of the corporate supply chain that works in much the same way.

First stores. You need to meet with buyers. These are the gate-keepers to the shelves that you want to put your precious products on. Buyers are like the world's greatest shoppers. They shop for shoppers and they shop for shops. Too much use of the word shop? I think so.

Let me explain it better. If you are a massive chain store, then you employ people whose job it is to buy goods for you to sell on to the public.

Now a great buyer is more than a person who can bulk buy from people like you. They have a tough task of finding products that do many things:

- Meet the quality standard of the store
- Meet the ethos of the brand

- Meet the legal or policy requirements of the store's supply chain commitments. Put simply, this means not buying from sweatshops if they promised not to. Checking for modern slavery and suchlike
- Match what shoppers expect to see in that store
- Meet the demand that there will be at the right time. Tough job when buyers do their shopping at least a season ahead. How else are Easter eggs on the shelves on 1st January?
- Sell well
- Give them a competitive advantage over other stores
- Make a profit.
- Enhance the brand reputation

Direct to corporates

There are, of course, products that are just consumed by corporates. Someone has got to supply them and I can't think of a better person than you.

Products can be tougher to get in front of corporates and using your network to see who is willing to make an introduction for you is a really powerful way forward. I have been approached by some product businesses when I was in corporate. Some I could not make the introduction for, but many I was very happy to do so, especially when I could see the potential in the product for a part of my company.

Be prepared to offer out some of your products if you can and let people see the benefits.

You should also be seriously considering trade shows and fairs. Like I have already said, you may want to go to some in research mode before committing to be an exhibitor. If you are going to book, make sure to ask questions of the organisers about the attendees. What job titles do they have? How many tick the box that say that they have authority to purchase? Do they work in the companies that you want to sell to?

It goes without saying that whether you are in products or service, you are going to benefit from having a quality digital presence and we will look at that in more detail in Chapter 9 - Articulate Your Offer.

7

OVERCOME YOUR DOUBTS

You, my friend, are amazing, and I am going to explain to you why you are amazing and why you 100% deserve to have those corporate contracts. There is no one better to fill that gap in the middle than you. In fact, when I peer into that gap, what I see is the shape of you. You are the missing jigsaw piece. As the gears of those corporate behemoths start to grind dry, you're the delightful juicy oil that is going to lubricate them.

I was going to say we will feed the beast with you but that sounds like you are a sacrifice to the Minotaur and quite frankly, I do not agree with human sacrifices. I love the Minoans even though they were reputedly feeding young folks to the Minotaur. A wonderful people who started what we now know as Western Civilisation. I am not often speechless but when I went to Knossos Palace, I was. It is in a beautiful spot. That place had some sort of psycho geographic effect on me. Knowing that the world I live in and the ways we live, what we see as civilisation all started there, combined with it as the home of one of the most famous Greek myths was overwhelming.

The sense of history along with the fact that this is a real place and is the real home of the Minoan people and reputed home of the Minotaur (probably not real but a great story of a half man half bull creature). What on earth they were thinking of feeding lovely young folks to bulls is quite beyond me, but they built a lovely palace in quite a beautiful spot and used infrastructure engineering solutions that would take us hundreds of years to rediscover.

So, to summarise, we won't say feed the beast. It is too angry and blood thirsty, but we will say close the gap.

There is a gap in the middle and it needs to close. The more it closes the better for all involved. You will have more corporate contracts. Corporates will have a more diverse supply chain and meet their SME targets. I will stop writing books about that and instead free all the monkeys from zoos or visit all the transit systems in my book. I will definitely go to Walton's Mountain, which is actually in Schuyler, Virginia. Basically, live the dream.

But I hear you. I hear you say what is stopping you.

When you read that list in Chapter 2, did one or more of those statements about why you can't do this leap out at you? Really? Well firstly, let me congratulate you. Why? Well, my dear friend and amazing reader, you read it, you identified with it, you read my invitation to you that said you can stop now, or you can stay on and do the hard work.

And guess what?

You stayed.

Through the hard work, the digressions, the geography and the classical history references

You stayed through them all.

Why?

Because you have two things. One, you have hope and two, you have the belief that you can change. You know what is the easiest thing we can change together? It is your mind.

Hope is the essential spirit that humans need to survive what can, at times, be a challenging and difficult world. Hope is the essence of spirit that entrepreneurs need when they step into that world of uncertainty that is starting a business. You have it. The quantity may bob up and down but you have it and it brought you here.

You also believe that you can change because you said 'yes, those are my challenges' and you stayed till now to get the help to change that mindset.

You are 50% of the way to changing. In the words of Henry Ford, if you think you can or think you can't, you are probably right.

We are going to take a good look at each of these reasons why you shouldn't work with corporate and demolish them one at a time. Now we are going to do a pretty thorough job of this right now. However, you need to keep the work going so before we start, let's look at how some of those ideas got in there in the first place.

Gremlins. Some of us remember Gremlins as an 80s kids' film about cute fluffy creatures who, if they are cared for wrongly, turn nasty and evil. Basically, you cannot feed a Gremlin after midnight. Now, I have met many a wonderful person who has Gremlins in their brain. Gremlins who have been fed after midnight and turned nasty. Now they are living in their heads, telling them lies. Sometimes those lies are meant to keep them small and sometimes they are meant to keep them safe. But they are lies all the same. Sometimes, the lies started as the words of others. People with good intent and people with bad intent, all jumbled into a big pack of lies that the Gremlins can send out into your brain whenever you want to make progress or try something new or scary or play bigger than you feel right now.

Who put the words into those lies that your gremlins tell you? What was their intent? What was their impact? Who fed your Gremlin? You see, brain Gremlins cannot be fed. Ever. Not even before midnight.

Maybe your friends or family are scared you will fail and feel the pain of that. They may well want to protect you from that. Keep you safe from harm. What if we flip that and by not even trying to win those contracts that you want, you are working more and harder than you must. Or are you doing work that you don't want to because the work you do want is behind those corporate doors? Then that is a reactive form of safety that is keeping you safe in the moment but not in the long term.

Think of it like this. You want a Gremlin to call out if you are about to cross the road and there is traffic coming. Great, thanks Gremlin, I didn't get knocked down by that car. I will look again and cross safely. You don't want the Gremlins telling you never to cross roads. That will be inhibiting.

Whilst I am the very person who would love to help you plan a journey that involves never crossing a road, I do think that the adventure will be somewhat short and limited. What you want is to acknowledge that there could be some disappointment – you might not win every contract or every client, but you don't want to get none because you never crossed that road to see what might be there for you.

Perhaps the people feeding the Gremlins those words worry that you will succeed and leave them behind. I'm going to be honest with you right here, you might and you might not. You will keep the ones you value, who value you, and over time, they will learn that you are not leaving them. The others? Well, I think you and I can see that is a problem that will resolve itself.

Can we pause and have a word about people who tell you 'You've changed'?

I have some responses that you are welcome to plagiarise. Some of these are already plagiarised:

'Why, thank you for noticing'

'I know, I have been working hard on myself'

'Thank you, that was my plan'

'We are supposed to'

'Yes, I'm enjoy my personal or professional growth'

Add your own, share them and send me an email with them.

Beware anyone who notices positive changes in you and tries to turn them into a negative. Whatever is happening with them must be about them and not you.

Leave them to it and do not let them feed the Gremlins.

Are there people who envy you who fed some words to the Gremlins so that you wouldn't outdo them? Envy is one of the most destructive emotions I have ever witnessed in others. It is a poison in the heart. I have empathy and sympathy for those who are driven by envy.

I see them destroy relationships in their own lives and I see that they miss out on something so precious. The joy of seeing someone you care for you do well, succeed, achieve, be happy or whatever it is. And you feel joy for them. I find that an uplifting and joyful experience. Like you were on their team the whole time, even if you just had your pom-poms out to cheer lead them and by golly, they have won, and you are on your feet cheering in your heart and soul. Your emotions rise with them and you feel so happy.

Now imagine that you see that happen and as you try to feel that joy, what you feel is envy. You wish it was you and not them, you wish they had less or had struggled more to get it. You pick away every part of their joy or success, gnawing at each bone until you find a flaw. Desperate to find a way to bring a negative into it. You get out your big straw and you suck the joy out of it as hard as you can. Maybe even discreetly using that passive aggressive put down that you cast off as 'just a joke' when you see the hurt or appalled look on their face.

Perhaps you curl up inside behind a plastered smile because you want to be joyful about it. Maybe you adore this person and you really are pleased for them. But deep down you feel somehow that them having that is stopping you from having that. Maybe you didn't even want it or work for it but now you see them with it, you covet it. You feel somehow them getting it is what is detracting you from having it.

Perhaps the guilt of that feeling eats you up and you wonder why you can't just be happy for the other person.

I see those people and, as I say, I have sympathy and empathy. I never want that coldness to grasp at me and I don't want that envious guilt either. I also avoid those people. Energy vampires are not my tribe. So, I see them, and I say I know that what is happening to you comes from a dark place that is causing pain. I empathise and I sympathise. Now do the work, do the work that you must do on you to change that. Do whatever needs to be done to take yourself into a place where you can pop on those pom-poms and cheer along with the rest of us.

Here is what I am advising you. Those people with the envy are not allowed to feed your Gremlins. Ever. Envy is potent and toxic and you, my amazing entrepreneur, have worked too damn hard and too smart to let it give snacks to your Gremlins. So, sift through those statements that got in there from a place of envy, recognise them for what they are and get rid of them. We are not having those.

I want you to remember that when you hear them in future and choose to change what they say or ignore it. Do not pass the snack to the Gremlins.

Now we have explored why some of the limiting phrases might be in there and who put them there, let's look at what the statements are and just knock 'em dead.

I'm just not corporate

No one was born corporate. Also, what does 'corporate' really mean? It is just a concept; it is not a real thing. I have had people say it to me as a compliment and as a veiled insult... Albeit, a flimsy veil!

It is also such a spectrum. From the outside it may look like it is one 'type' of thing, but I promise you, it isn't. Corporate varies from one place to another. Corporate at Google looks quite different to corporate at Lloyds.

I notice this all the time when I am in large corporate buildings which are shared. I'm a bit of an anthropologist at heart, or maybe I'm nosy and curious. I love when you are taking a lift though a high building and the lift pops open at different floors with different firms in them and you get a brief glimpse of their corporate veneer. You get a 30 second flash of the differences.

I used to often go to a building where a well-known shirt maker had their corporate HQ. You could spot the staff in the lift as they were the impeccably tailored, hip, young people with ankle grazing suits trousers. Their floor screamed 'we have been making sharp shirts for years and we are young and vibrant'. I would be heading to an internal client's office which was a railway company that was styled a bit like the big brother house. The tribe, including myself were dressed, far more staid and the office was much more generic big company office style.

Both big corporates and totally different.

I remember going for training on business cases in a high-profile law firm's office in the Waterloo area of London. Rather nice premises in Buckingham Palace Road. My colleague and I headed into the shared building and it was quite the spectacle. Not the law firm. These are pretty much styled the same the world over, from what I have seen so far. Sharp, crisp edges, greys, monochromes, accent colours but nothing whacky, expensive wood finishes, luscious and efficient. Always good coffee and decent biscuits. If you are paying top dollar legal fees, you have a bit of an expectation of how it will look, and I have never had that expectation challenged.

Next to this legal firm though was the Google London office. It looked exactly like everything I had imagined a Google office would. Bright colours, sofas, objects used as furniture, I think there was half a London bus somewhere, pop art, bright splashes of colours, wild patterns. You get the picture. I could work for Google, really, I could, as I know the reward that comes from pushing myself out of my comfort zone. But I would be out of my comfort zone for a while in that environment. I guess the jarring patterns would throw me for a while, but I would get there. I would adapt and I would learn the ways and I would evolve. If I walked into a big legal firm or finance house or utility company, I would stroll in there without batting an eyelid.

My point is, what you might perceive corporate to look, be or feel like, will have variations and you can choose to start with the one you feel is closest to your tribe if you need that comfort.

I suspect that you really don't though. Your brain might tell you that you do. Its job is to keep you alive, remember. You know what, though? You are not really a play-it-safe type. How do I know that? Well, you are an entrepreneur. By nature, a person willing to break from the crowd, do something different, set your own path in life and take risks. You are not rogue but you are not averse to a bit of risking not blending in.

I remember going to a conference in Birmingham at a big hotel. I worked for a railway company at the time. I wandered into the hotel and there were two conferences on that day.

There was a group of people, dressed smartly, quite colourful. A mix of sharp suits with shoes and sharp suits with trainers. The demographic was 20s to 40s age range and roughly 50/50 split between women and men.

There was another group. Again, wearing suits. Mostly black, brown and grey suits. Maybe one pair of trainers, but mostly shoes. Age range 40s to 60s and a gender split of about 85% men.

As I was walking through the lobby, a very helpful young man working at the hotel stepped forward and asked:

'Can I help direct you today?'

Without even thinking, I said:

'Thank you, I can see where my people are' and I headed off in my grey suit and shoes to the mostly middle-aged male group. I am not bashing the railway company at all as they are a company who have worked hard to redress the gender balance that has been baked in over many years. I share this to illustrate that even what you think 'looks, sounds, or feels corporate', it is such a variety that you can start to dismantle it from looking a certain way.

I hated working in corporate

This one could be a little trickier. Especially if you have plastered it all over your social media. If you are rampant anti-corporate, you do need to ask yourself why you want to win work with them. If it is to exercise some demons or prove someone wrong, that might be cathartic. I am not judging. Not a bit as I once did an excellent piece of work in corporate, fuelled by the knowledge that someone thought I couldn't do it. My goodness, I worked my socks off to show that I could do a great job. Partly because, deep down, I wasn't sure I could do it either at the time. All I am suggesting is that you look at whether that is a good enough reason and will you enjoy the work as much as the victory. If not, maybe look at the alternatives.

Now, there is a great side to 'I hated working in corporate' that you can turn into your favour. If one of the reasons you want to work in corporate is because you can solve the problem that made your corporate life so awful, then go for it. If you hated working in corporate but are motivated to take what you offer into corporate and improve it for offers, and make yourself some money along the way, then good for you. Do not let that experience hold you back.

Also, you may find that you have a different experience. I worked at one corporate that I did not enjoy years ago. It put me off that whole industry. It is only years later that I would now consider doing any work with any corporate in that industry. Even then, I would make sure to check in with myself that if I wasn't loving it, I would exit from that industry and leave it alone in future. Some places are just not for you and that is ok.

They won't want someone like me

Oh, I hear that. What is it that you think is so different or wrong with you? What makes you feel so "other" that you don't think they want you?

Did a Gremlin feed you that? Or is that you who fed this Gremlin? Is your brain trying to save you from being rejected? That is, after all, our deepest human fear. Rejection meant death in prehistoric times, so it is not a primal fear based on a fate worse than death. It is a fear based on death, except we probably accept death as inevitable eventuality, whilst rejection we can try to avoid.

If I had fairy dust to sprinkle on you and protect you from feeling the pain or fear of rejection then I would. I do not have that fairy dust. You do not need it. I will give you something more powerful and potent. Knowledge. I was going to say a secret, but secrets are often used by bullies as a power tool to choose who to include and who to exclude. I detest those working environments, so I am not going to use it as a literary tool. I have shared some of my personal secrets with you but that is about showing you some vulnerability and building trust so that you will take the actions, not controlling who gets what useful knowledge.

So, here is the potent knowledge you need. Those people in that corporate world. You see them? Well, every one of them has the same primal fears as you. That is how primal fears work. We don't get to choose their existence, only how we manage and respond to them.

So, they are all in that huge tribe and deep down, they have that rejection fear too. Now, some of them have done the work and they are all over it. Some of them are paralysed by it and some are middling along, doing ok, knowing it might pop up from time to time.

Remember our "corporate world is like a small city" analogy? Well, these days, corporates are becoming more diverse. Some evolve faster than others. What that does mean is that there are all types of people in them. People like me, people like you, people different from either of us. A great big jumble of different types of people. No better and no worse than you or I. Some of those people have SME targets to meet and, when you turn up in your SME shape, which may indeed be a bit different from their corporate shape, they are going to be delighted to see you.

Which takes me to our next two demons:

- I don't fit in there.
- I don't look, sound, think, dress [add your own self bashing words here] like them.

I am also going to tell you why you either do fit in or don't have to fit. Either way, you are going to feel more at ease in corporate environments. There are no false promises in this book, so you are unlikely to read this book, dash into Savile Row shouting 'suit me up', and saunter through Canary Wharf offices like you owned them as soon as you reach the back cover. If you do, drop me an email first as I love taking the driverless trains or the clipper boats down to Canary Wharf. I'll keep you company and I have some clients down there I can visit whilst you take the place by storm.

What you will feel is more confidence about being in those environments and confidence is a journey, not an end goal, so that confidence will grow and grow endlessly.

There are two options to choose from, so you can choose your own adventure here. You can choose to fit and feel comfortable – excellent choice.

Or

You can choose to be comfortable not fitting in – also an excellent choice.

They are your choices to make, and no one gets to make that choice for you. If you are struggling with that choice, it is one to mull over and work with a coach to help you. Don't ask your friends and family as their advice may come from a place of love (or maybe not) but it is subjective and cannot help you get to the depths of how you really feel and what will work for you.

You see, the choice depends on you.

Let me tell you about my friend. She is highly creative, imaginative, sensitive, a polymath with a new passion every month. She is also hypersensitive to her environment and finds nuance a challenge in human behaviour.

She went along for an interview with a firm in a new industry. One known for conformance more than creativity. A place that does not scream out 'come here and be who you are' but 'come here and be like us'. It seemed a strange choice, but my friend was trying to challenge herself to make some life changes. So, off she went. She thought carefully about who they might want, how that type of person would answer and behave. The interview went well and out she came. But when we spoke, she was worried. You see, she didn't really enjoy being the person she had been in the interview. She was also worried about not getting the job because, you know – bills to pay. I asked her two questions. Do you want to become the person you were pretending to be?

Her answer was no.

Second question:

Are you able to keep up the pretense if you get the job?

Also, no.

So, for her, fitting in was not really an option that would sustain any sort of enjoyable life. When the job offer did come, she turned it down.

I had a different experience when I went from a small corporate job to a big one.

I went for the interview and it was a bit daunting. I felt a bit out of my depth but not in the wrong pool. I felt that the people I was seeing were people I wanted to learn from, be around and be more like.

That company invested in me over the coming years. They spent tens of thousands on my personal and professional development. They pushed, stretched, challenged and supported me until I was a version of myself, I recognised as an evolution of me. The change was revolutionary but the difference was evolutionary because I was not a different me. My values and my core were still me; I was just a better version of me and better at being me.

I realised along the way that we are all a work in progress and if we choose that mindset then it is a lot less punishing than trying to complete ourselves. Especially when we are all enough. We can be more, we can be different, and we can evolve but that is different to being incomplete, unfinished or broken.

The journey out of corporate and into owning my own business has meant that I have to choose some areas to work on and pick where my growth areas will be. But I am not waiting until I have done them to have what I want, and neither should you.

I'm not enough

This one is often referred to as imposter syndrome too. Guess what? Corporates are filled with people also wondering if they are not enough. There are also a number of people who are A LOT. Those people, so sure of themselves that they never seek anyone else's counsel, don't listen or ask for alternative views, love to have an echo chamber of accordant voices around them. Never worked with one? You are very lucky. They are abominable and dangerous. Personally, I think a little touch of self-doubt helps now and then, when you have big accountabilities, you need to look around and get other input. You need to know that you are not infallible and where your weakness lies. Not so you can work on them very hard but so that you can listen to other people, whose strengths lie in your areas of weakness. A little humility in this area goes a long way to making you a rounded human that people want to deal with. You are already enough. You do not need to be everything to all people. Just keep away from the end of the 'I'm not enough' spectrum that stops you doing this work. You are enough, you're amazing.

I will also share with you that the very best of the senior leaders that I have ever worked with are the ones who have enough humility to at times check in on themselves. To have those doubts of 'Am I up to this task?' The ones who don't tend to create brutal working environments where mistakes are made and blame assigned, people are put at risk of harm and creativity and innovation are at rock bottom. Any creative or innovative environment must allow room for doubt and errors. Only those who can have a comfortable, controlled and productive amount of self-doubt can create those workplaces.

I'm too much

Are you really? Or is someone feeding that Gremlin because you are highlighting their feelings of not enough-ness? There we go, Chapter 7 and I'm just making up words now.

They are too much

Have you looked at a place after doing the research and thought 'I am appalled at working there, it is too much?' Pick another one and start researching them then.

But first... check that you are not caught in feeling like you are not enough.

What if I get the work but can't meet the expectation?

This one has two facets. One is volume. What if you get a massive order and you cannot fulfill it? You simply must be realistic when you put your proposal together about how many hours or how much quantity you are able to provide. If winning a contract is going to mean a huge step up in your output, then you must have made sure in advance that you can do that.

What will it take for you to deliver it? Can you or your manufacturer or logistics company meet the level of demand? Are you offering more hours in the week than you have? How can you create those hours? Do you need associates, more employees, a PA? Figure it out and plan for it so that if you win the work, you can deliver it. This is not happening to you. You want this and you oversee this and need to take steps so that if it happens, you can do it.

No one would pay me that day rate for what I can do

Yes, they would, and they do. Get used to being paid what you are worth. You will love it and you deserve it. That's it. You are worth being paid your worth.

The market is already too crowded.)This one makes me want to weep, remember all those missed targets?)

If there was no space for you in the market, then the targets would already be met. Governments and their supply chains, which often include the largest corporates, would all be boasting about how they spend a third of their annual spend with SMES. You would be sick of hearing about it. Oops, no you wouldn't be because you would have a healthy pipeline of corporate work so actually, you would be rather pleased.

Remember, that is not what they are doing. They are moving the targets, trying to meet them and you are keen to do the work and there is still that huge gap in the middle.

Today is the day you stop feeding the Gremlins and you cut off everyone else's access to Gremlins. I care not about the intent of the people who are feeding them. The impact is that they are holding you back and you are done with that. You have already built a business. Taken a little acorn and grown it. Maybe it is a whip or a sapling right now. You are now going to make it into a mighty oak, as splendid, strong and super as you, rooted in what you already know how to do and branching out into a new space.

Remember that you, my friend, are amazing.

I promised you a trick to deal with Gremlins. Everything you need to get rid of them is with you.

Every time you notice a Gremlin raising its hideous head, you are going to do two things:

- Come back to this chapter and exorcise it
- Read your vision and your why to remind yourself why you are doing this

8

REFINE YOUR STRATEGY

I n this chapter, you are going to consider your strategy for getting into working with corporate and creating and nurturing a pipeline of corporate work. You will also start to plan how you will implement that strategy and what tactics you will use.

Strategy

Strategy happens at three main levels within a business if you are a small to medium business. The first is corporate level, where you make decisions about what type of business you are in, who you will sell to, how you will fund your business, what are the marketplaces you are in.

The next level down is business level, where you make decisions about how you will generate this year's income, how much turnover you want to make, will you grow, stabilise or contract this year?

Third level is operational. Will you find new suppliers, change your quality or pricing, look for a manufacturer with a lower cost? How will you continuously improve your day-to-day operations? All the issues that occur and impact at the front line.

Whether you are already doing corporate work or not, deciding to create a pipeline of corporate work is a corporate level strategy decision. The reason is that this will change the nature of your business if you predominantly work business-to-consumer. Please don't panic if you are thinking that you love selling direct to consumers and you are great at it. You are not going to lose that and in fact, the skills you use for that have put you in good stead for business-to-business selling. Adding a business-to-business line is a big decision to make and will take effort, planning, resources and enthusiasm, so you want to make it at corporate level.

You see, I know the mindset of entrepreneurs. Massive ideas generators who love a shiny new project and will follow like a puppy chasing a bouncing ball. Except puppies have boundless energy. Hang on, that is also many of the entrepreneurs I know. I know why I started this analogy - it is because puppies have little else to do than bound around being cute puppies, chewing up stuff and taking extensive naps, which their owners photograph and put on social media. Most entrepreneurs I know find it hard enough to find time to eat healthily, never mind nap. As for the viral photos of cute entrepreneurs napping, well let me know when you find it.

My point is, this falls into the category of give it some serious consideration and if you are going to do this (I am going to assume you are, as we are at Chapter 8 now) then you put this into your corporate level strategy. You plan for it; you resource it and you do it properly and then you email me and tell me how amazing you are doing. Honestly, if you want someone to read your email, cheer for you and write back with pure joy then send me those emails.

Your strategy is basically that you are going to follow the steps in this book in sequence and then implement them. Sounds easy? Well, it is straightforward. I mean, I am not going to come round and do it for you. No one is and why would we because remember we went over how awesome you are? How unique and interesting you are and how corporates can't wait to have a piece off you? Well, it only works if you implement it, so that is what you are going to do.

Fundamental questions to answer are below:

- When will you start? Be realistic here. If you are about to launch another major project, product or transformation within your business, is this the right time to also start going after corporate work?
- If it's not, it doesn't mean you have to postpone the whole thing but maybe you don't dive straight in. You space out doing the research or you outsource some of the elements.
- How will you resource this with time and money?
- Who will do this? You, a business development or sales team?
- Where will you start? This should be your first target client.
- Pipeline – could you consider even just starting to plan this?

Tactics

I'm going to be bold and tell you that there is no better tactical approach to getting this done than using a project management approach. There may be some fancy schmancy new techniques out there but, call me old fashioned or even basic if you are down with the kids (my son assures me that anyone who still uses this phrase is anything but down with the kids), but the best approach to managing projects is still project management.

The elements of starting with the end in mind, breaking it into smaller tasks that all add up to the end goal. Working out the time, people and costs resources needed for each task and for the task of overseeing it all. You cannot beat a good solid project management plan with scope, work breakdown structure, cost plan, resource plan and a decent schedule, which includes some float.

Actually, you can beat it. You know how you beat it? With changes. Unmanaged, uncontrolled, unplanned chaotic changes. So, you also need some basic change control principles. Now, don't lose your rag and the will to live here. You might be thinking that now I am asking you to become a trained project manager to do all of this.

Sit right back down and hold on to that rag. For I might not be a fairy godmother - the outfits are too frilly for me and I'm too pragmatic for magic - I am, however, of more practical use to you for I am a trained project manager and I have set out below a nice simple project plan concept that you can use to write up your tactical approach to implement.

If you want a free download of that, you can also pop onto my website and download it.

I have also included 5 key questions for you to ask on change control so that this project:

- Gets done
- Delivers the benefits you need

You see, projects are about delivering benefits, not about keeping project managers in work.

The 5 key principles of change control for you are:

When you make a change to your plans ask these questions:

- What impact does this change have on the time taken to start winning corporate work?
- What impact does this change have on the costs involved?
- What impact does this change have on the benefits of winning corporate work?
- What are the consequences of making this change?
- What is driving me to consider making this change?

Project Management for entrepreneurs

On this table, list out all of your current projects by what stage they are at. You must include here your project to get into working with corporates and building a pipeline of corporate work.

Ideas and concepts All the ideas or concepts for projects	Projects in research Projects you are researching the benefits, time, cost, resources, viability
Projects in action Projects which you have started	Projects completing Projects which are close to completion. Note: the last 5% of any projects takes an exponential level of effort to close out properly. Close out should include assessing if this is achieved, what you set out to achieve. Did it deliver the benefits?

Project Plan

The 5 key elements here you want to remember are:

- Benefits - that is why you are doing this. If they are gone, do not be afraid to stop or cancel your project.
- Scope - what you are doing and everything on the task breakdown.
- Cost - £££ - how much you are planning to spend on this project.
- Time - how long it will take from now until completion.
- Quality - how good you want this to be.

Once you have established these, you want to regularly check on them. They are all intrinsically linked from now on and when one changes, so do the others.

Benefits – list here the benefits of having a corporate pipeline	Task Breakdown – List here all of the tasks that need to be undertaken	Resource breakdown – list here all of resources that you will need to undertake each task including people.	Cost breakdown – List here all of the costs involved	Time – when I will start & how long will it take?
Higher rates for work More secure income	Networking	Time to attend events Travel to events Business cards	£100	Start next week – ongoing activity
	Update LinkedIn profile	Time & laptop Proposal		Next Tuesday – 3 hours

You can add rows and columns to fit the categories that are relevant to your business and start to populate this and use it to track progress because what gets measured, gets done.

Now you will see that I pre-populated your project plan with networking as one of your activities.

My network is a huge part of my business success and I know, without a doubt, it can be yours.

You might want to read another book about networking. There are books on networking for extroverts, networking for introverts, networking for neurodivergences, networking in other cultures, languages, networking for vegans, networking for goldfish owners. I haven't read that last one yet but I'm sure it is out there somewhere.

I run some networking classes myself.

There is so much advice on networking that I don't plan to replicate it here, but I will give you some specific advice on networking if you want to get into working with corporates.

You must do it.

That's my advice.

People do business with people and you are your best asset.

Now, your business might be online, and all your networking might also be online and that is fine.

Networking is a spectrum of quality. At the bottom end of that spectrum is the speed dating approach of exchanging details rapidly with a whole room, swapping business cards or leaflets and trying to pretend there is no agenda.

Top of the range is having some conversations to meet and start to get to know people on an open basis. By open, what I mean is that you both know that you are networking. You recognise that maybe one day you will be of use to each other and in the moment, you both set that aside and just meet each other as humans and engage in being humans for a bit.

You see, humans are tribal. Our need for others is primal. So, it is ok to know that and explore each other on that basis.

Let me tell you about some situations I have encountered.

I was having an event for some clients and collaborators. One of my clients, May, called me on the day and said that she had just met with someone at one of her corporate clients. The guy, Joe, was thinking of moving jobs and, as I have a large network in the field he works in, May was wondering if she could invite

Joe along. She had told Joe that I would be a good person to ask about opportunities and that I could probably introduce him to some people. I told her to extend the invite and I would see her that night. Along popped Joe, introduced himself to me and said he felt a little awkward, but May had said to come along and mention to me he was thinking of changing jobs. I was 100% fine with that. Totally open discussion, no hidden agenda and I was happy to arrange to introduce him to some people and have future chats. My corporate clients often ask me if I know people for certain roles so that was very appropriate.

A few months before that, I had a call from an old colleague. He was thinking of changing jobs and said that in the industry we had both worked, he didn't know anyone with a bigger network, so he thought of ringing me and asking me for some advice and help. I really rated this guy in his role and suggested various places he would be a great fit. A few weeks later I recommended him to some head-hunters who were working for one of my clients for a major international role.

I am 100% okay being approached and asked to help. Does that mean I will indiscriminately recommend everyone who approaches me? Absolutely not. You see, I have mastered the use of the word "No". I am less comfortable saying no than yes to a request for help, but I am more comfortable saying I cannot help you than agreeing to help someone when either I don't want to or cannot really be of any help to.

Here is what doesn't work for me though. Someone pretending they don't have an agenda, trying to 'work' me and then manoeuvre or manipulate me into helping them. My radar is pretty good for this and I will spot it quickly. I know a lot of other people who also have excellent radars for this.

When I was in the corporate where I started, and rose through the ranks, I saw some real eye-opening behaviour that helped turn that radar from a few butterflies in my stomach or hairs standing up my neck into a full-on siren going off in my head.

Remember how I said that a large corporate is like a small town. In every small town there are people you do want to be around and people you cross the road to avoid. The people I do want to be around are those who hear you are going for promotion, encourage you, congratulate you when you get it and treat you the same as before. Those are my people and that is my tribe.

Then there are the people who say 'I never thought you would get that job, but well done'. Hmm.

But the people who make my siren go off can best be represented by these two people. One we shall call Pearl. Pearl and I worked on the same floor for about 6 years. We were both early to start and late to finish workers. We had a shared kitchen on that floor and would often bump into each other in there. I would say hello and she would say... nothing. Not a word, not a smile.

Now, only people working for that company would ever be in there, so it was clear that we worked in the same company. At one point, we had to have some discussions about a piece of work. She was courteous and polite but still in the lift, in the kitchen, wherever I would say hello or good morning, still, she would say nothing.

And then, one glorious morning, I won her over. Pearl strolled into the kitchen as I was making coffee and said, 'Good morning'.

I played it cool - trust me, I was so cool I said, 'good morning'. What do you make of that for a reply? I will admit that I said it with the energy of a puppy, but I think it was cool enough.

I was pleased. I knew then that she had just needed time. She just wasn't ready for me before. Damn me and my friendliness, couldn't I just be a little patient with the introverts. I'm married to one, I know they need some space.

She just needed 6 years of me saying good morning approximately once a week. That's only around 276 hellos / good mornings I had invested. I went swanning back to my desk and told one of my colleagues 'Pearl just said good morning to me. You said I was wasting my time being friendly to her, but 6 years and she finally said good morning.'

'Toughest project you've delivered yet' he wittily replied. How we laughed. That is until my boss chimed in 'Pearl? Pearl x? She is saying good morning to you because it was announced that you got promoted. She only speaks to people who are at your new job grade and above.'

'Oh, she's a Fred then?

Yes, she's a Fred.

Reader, I have not lost my mind and started writing fiction prose mid business book. You see a Fred was a very special type of person. Named after a chap who was called... yes, you've guessed it, Fred. His special talent was to walk along any of the floors in the building and say hello by name to anyone who was his job grade and above, deemed as important by Fred.

Except for the Personal Assistants to Important People, the rest of that floor would be completely ignored. What was quite so special was his level of blatantness at this. He would call right across the heads of all the people he had decided were unimportant, right over to Important People strolling by, like it was totally natural.

I found it hilarious.

I found it hilarious as it was like walking through a small-town shouting about what a terrible human you are. Advertising to the world that you greet people by hierarchy.

Those are not my people. I am not their person. I am happy not to be a part of their tribe.

The day I heard Fred say at a conference that the key to successful projects is how you lead your team I almost fell off my chair laughing. I mean, it is true, but I had never seen a man more open about having an agenda.

So, there may be a place in my network for Fred and Pearl, but there is no warmth, I am never going to recommend them, introduce them to people or do anything that is not my professional duty to help them.

So, make it nice and genuine and people based and collaborative.

I build my network by focusing 100% on the relationships first. I knew when I started my business that there would be people it would be great to meet and tell them what I was doing, as they would be able to either put work my way or recommend me to others. So, I contacted them and made plans to meet. I was open about what I was doing but I put my energy into building a relationship with them, not working an angle on them.

That has been my same approach through my corporate career and translating it over to my own business has been highly successful. If we build a relationship and no workflows from that, I consider that as successful as when the work does flow. That is a people first approach.

You will get back what you put out there. If you are putting out people based, genuine and collaborative approaches, that is what you will attract. Of course, the variety of people means that some of those relationships will be more transactional than others. You must meet people where they are at. Not everyone wants to be in environments to hang out, their comfortable space might be quite business-like. It is about acceptance of their approach and needs.

As you develop your pipeline, this is a highly effective way to initiate those new relationships with businesses you want to bring into your pipeline. Create relationships with people in those businesses and tend to those relationships.

If you are relationship first, business second, you cannot lose in the long term.

The interpersonal part is very organic. Relationships will develop over time and people will become clients at different rates. That is your pipeline starting to work. Whilst the relationship has to be organic, you do have to have some systematic approaches as you cannot spend your entire life at events and network building without it being managed. That is about resource management and a world away from working an angle on someone.

How you will resource manage this is fairly simple to start with.

Some questions to get you going:

- Who will you aim to work with?
- When would you like to work with them? Now or in future years?
- How will you manage your business development?
- Are you going to do business development or is it someone in your team?
- How much time are you going to spend on this?
- How much money do you need to invest in this?
- Who do you know?
- Who do you need to get to know?

You can buy a system called a customer relationship management (CRM system) or you can get basic access to some of them for free.

This is too much to keep in your head if you want to have a pipeline as you will eventually lose track of it or become overwhelmed.

So, either get a CRM or use your own system.

I have included a simple chart here that you can use to get you started. You can download this template from my website for free.

Potential client	Existing client	Named contact	Contact details	Last contact Date	Any agreed follow up	Planned next contact date	Method – email / call / coffee/ lunch (Note any preference they have)	Networking events

A full CRM will give you the space to record all sorts of details. What is happening in that person's life, their kid's birthday, favourite dog breed etc. It really is up to you how much you record and how you use it.

If your natural personality type is cringing about talking about people's kids and dogs, find your own way with relationship building. That does not mean do not do it of course!

Write it down, put it in your schedule, like I have said. If you have it on your plan and you need to change or move it, make sure you swap it for another day rather than just remove it. If you plan to call four contacts next month, put a 15- or 30-minute slot in your diary saying 'call x'

That way it doesn't drift.

Only remove anything if you have done the activity already or some other activity that created the result you need. This is fundamental to properly controlling change.

9

ARTICULATE YOUR OFFER

W hat a place you are at now. I'm amazed at you. I'm not surprised though as we established your amazingness right at the start. We have come a long way since Chapter 1.

You now know:

- Why you want to work with corporates
- Why they should work with you
- What your vision for your work and business life is
- You now have:
- Research about your potential clients
- A well-defined proposal
- A belief that you can do this
- A strategy to incorporate this into your business and life

Now you just need to be able to tell the right people about this in the right way.

Did you think we could keep this between us? Come on now, we both know that isn't going to work.

Let's start with a bit of an audit of what you already have. I'm all about productivity, which means not reinventing wheels. If we can just reshape existing wheels, that is better. Except wheels need to be round, so that analogy sort of falls over. You get the gist.

What assets do you have right now that set out your offer? This could include:

- Your products
- Brochures
- Leaflets
- Sales page
- Website
- LinkedIn profile
- Emails
- Books
- Photographs
- Videos
- Written proposals
- Interpretive dance – (I'm still hoping someone goes for this, except maybe your offer is an interpretive dance, in which case you must find another way to articulate it as you can't just give away the goods.)

Can any of these either be used as they are or adapted for your new corporate market? Adapt what you have that works. If the effort is too great, just start from fresh.

Remember that the language you will use is different from that you might have used selling to consumers.

If you have nothing on this list, then that is ok too. You can just get started now. You will not need everything on that list, but you will need some because you really are ready now to start telling people about your offer.

Did you just take a massive gulp or hear a Gremlin trying to raise its voice?

Remember, they are waiting for you. Those behemoths that you think are faceless. They are filled with sad faces of people just like me. Sad because they have met every other target: stretch targets, lean targets, KPIs... all sorts of hard, tricky stuff, mega projects - on time and on budget. What is making the sad face? The fact that they cannot hit their SME targets. The gap in the middle is still there. And you are ready. You have come this far. Now you just need to be able to bring them the good news and turn their frowns upside down.

How will those people know what you offer? Write a list of ways that you will show people what you offer. You can use the list above to start. LinkedIn is a great one to start with, it is free, heavily used by the corporate market and you can look at other people's profiles for ideas and inspiration. Set yourself up a personal page and a business page and link them to each other.

If you are looking at other people for inspiration, look at people who run businesses. Especially those who do business-to-business. The style and information is different from those who are employees and are putting their career history out to attract job offers.

Now, what else do you want to have? I would recommend a short brochure, even if it is a couple of pages. You want to get this down on paper, even if it is virtual paper i.e., a laptop. Write down what you offer so that you can see it laid out. Pricing, services, products, what is involved, some information about you.

Take your proposition from Chapter 6 - Proposal Definition, and flesh it out. Give it some life. Describe the benefits. My warning to you is not to get lost here in flowery language or the elements that you love to deliver. Remember to keep this tightly aligned to the corporates you are aiming to work with. Read over the research on their objectives. Look at the type of language that is used and what they are looking for. How do your benefits align to what they want?

The reason to write all this out is that you want to have some materials to show people when you take it to market. You also want to be able to distribute and take it with you so that you always have it when you are ready to do the talking.

If you are likely to be feeling awkward the first few times you are having these conversations, I can share a tip with you. I have a client who's fear reaction is freeze. So, when she is nervous, she freezes, her mind goes blank and she feels like every word she ever knew has packed up and left her brain. For her, we talked about how she can use a leaflet as a prop for her to read from. She has practiced doing it quite casually. She shows it to the person she is talking to and they both look through it, but she has the words right there on the page.

She had to make the brochure very attractive, with some great photographs that appeal to her client, so that it does catch their eye and they want to look. She has found this works well. The words are running away from her less often now because she knows she has them in her hand and the fact that the client is looking at that leaflet - and not at her eyes as she panics - is helping her relax whilst getting into the swing of talking. She can then put it away and revert to good eye contact and breathing and being her awesome self. I know that eventually she will not need that brochure. Her Gremlins are starving and soon they will have faded and gone.

Once you have your offer written out in this way, you are going to find a quiet, private space and read it out loud to yourself.

Say it. Say it again. Come on now, say it loud.

It can feel a bit uncomfortable and awkward starting to talk about your offer in this way. If you feel awkward about the corporate wording style because either it is new to you or you are used to the more personal style of selling to consumers, remember - you are still going to speak to people using your own natural talking style when you meet them, but you will have to be able to talk about you offer in the that way you have written it down.

The point of this is to get familiar with describing what you offer out loud. Not in your head because that is quite different. Some of the best presentations I ever wrote in my head fell apart the minute I gave voice to them. That is great. You know why? It is because I would never be saying it out loud for the first time to a room full of people. So, I knew it right away and re-worked them until they did work.

Sometimes what you have in your head or even written down, when you start to say it, you know it doesn't come across well or it is not you. So that is why we rehearse now and get it right. Then we don't have to walk away saying 'I wish I had said x, y, z instead'.

There is an expectation of a level of polish at corporate and that will come to you with practice and getting comfortable with articulating your own offer.

The part that a lot of entrepreneurs tell me they hate saying out loud is their price. A lot of people have said these:

- I mumble or look away when I have to say the price
- I hate saying the price
- I feel great talking about what I sell until I have to say the price
- I feel really exposed when I need to say price
- I have a price in my head and when they ask me, I drop that price or say I will get back to them

I have also observed people justify or apologise for their prices when asked. If you aren't confident in saying your price to a client, how do you expect them to feel confident about paying for it?

Now, here I do have a bit of a magic wand. Here is the discipline that you are going to get into. When someone asks you your price, you answer with a number.

Always, 100% of the time, a number.

The first word out of your mouth must be a number.

No qualification, no explanation, no apology.

A number straight away.

If you need to follow that with per day, or it's £5 per item for 1 and £3 per item for orders over 100, that is fine, but the first word is always going to be a number.

Shall I tell you why? It is not a sales strategy or a marketing tip. It is not even some clever psychology mind trick. It is as simple as this. In all the years I worked in corporate, buying a lot of stuff - I mean a lot, millions upon millions then into billions - every time I asked a price, I expected to hear a number in response.

And every word between my question and the actual number frustrated or disengaged me a little more. Hit me with a number right between the eyes and then offer the details. The structuring, the bulk discounts, the breakdown, whatever you want to do, but for the love of all is that dear or holy to you, give me that number first.

Once you start doing this, I promise you that it will also get easier. The more often you say I charge £10 per item, £100 per hour, £1000 per hour, £5000 per hour... whatever the rate, the more often you say it and say it right out the gate, then the easier it becomes.

A lot of corporate folk who have roles buying, have a commercial or financial background. They are highly numerate and generally comfortable with numbers and with discussing them. They are not awkward about hearing your pricing. What they do expect though, like I did, is a numerical answer to a numerical question.

So 'how much?' always must be answered with a number. I might smile or be silent and calm when you answer how much with a narrative. That is because I am a polite person and aware that we may be about to enter a negotiation, so I am trained to not react emotionally in negotiations. What I am doing is screaming inside when I ask for a number and you answer with a narrative, an apology or a justification.

I also now know two things; you are not comfortable or confident in your price and I have the upper hand in driving that price down if I wish to do so. You have inadvertently just lowered your price in my eyes without meaning to.

This might sound harsh but business can, at times, be a tough world. When it comes to talking about your pricing, I really do suggest that you follow this advice as the best thing you can do is get out of your own way.

You see, even if you hit me with a price that was well within my budget, if you gave me a lot of room for doubt, I could still choose to try to push that down because I will have somewhere else my budget is tight.

On the other hand, if a corporate does not want to pay it or it is outside their budget and they have no headroom or alternative, they will not pay it. I need you to know that it doesn't reflect on you as a person. It is not because they don't like you or you are not worth it or not enough. There can be several business reasons that you might have your pricing awry, or they might not pay that rate (remember, others might). None of this is personal to them, so long as they are professional, which 90% of them will be. Therefore, what you are not going to do is turn any commercial rejection of your pricing into Gremlin food.

Feel that you are not ready to shout out loud what you do, how others benefit and what it costs? Hmm, I suspect some of you may be in the 'hell, yeah' category and some of you are currently retreating to the safety of under a blanket, corner of the room, wherever your hiding place is.

As well as suspecting, I also planned for it. You see, it is a little weird, isn't it? We all know a couple of people who are great at shouting in your face about how great they are but very few of us want to be around those people. I mean, some folk elect people like to be their leader in groups or even their president or prime minister, but that is a field where you get ahead by getting one over on anyone else you can. I love politics but I am not naive enough to think it's a fairy tale world. Maybe it is because fairy tales are also hugely divorced from the reality of most of our worlds.

You don't want to be one of those people that everyone avoids because their message gets lost in the noise. Neither do you want to those people I smiled at politely whilst internally screaming 'say a number, any number'. You want to be the person who can describe what you do, how it meets their needs and what it costs in a way that you are comfortable with and that engenders confidence in the person listening to you.

If I had a magic sentence that I could give to do that, I would. I don't. And I'm sorry that I don't. What I have instead is a magic trick. It is called private rehearsal. It's a very simple process.

- Write the words
- Say them out loud

- What do you trip over or don't like saying?
- Can you fix the wording?

Ok, now say that out loud. Once you have the words, you are going to say them out loud 10 times in a row. Each time say it a little louder until you are raising your voice but not quiet shouting.

Now start again, 10 more times but each time try a different tone.

Now in front of a mirror, with different expressions. The one you want to master is smiling. Not grinning like a Cheshire cat. Not awkward, embarrassed, smiling. But smiling like you are a professional person describing your service and what it costs to someone who is considering buying it from you.

Once you have that, you are going to record it on video or audio. That way you have it for every future time. Eventually, you might not need this, but it is handy to have to listen to before you go into a meeting if you either suffer from nerves, mind blanks or you have a neuro divergence that impacts on your recall from your short-term memory under pressure. You have it there on your phone to have a quick listen before you head in.

This is a bit like aversion therapy. The first time you say you charge £1000 per day feels very different from when you've said it the 1000th time. I promise you this is true. It also gets easier to say when people have paid you that for delivering a service.

Working out pricing can be a little tricky as you don't want to start too low, and you don't want to price yourself out of every job. If that is what is going on and it's tricky then follow my advice in this chapter and give it a bit of trial and error.

If what keeps coming up for you is that you think you are not worth that amount, then I give you a piece of excellent advice. Get out of your own way and out of your own head. There, all better? No. Well what I suggest is that you consider two things:

If you are being paid for a product you already know what it costs to make and everything that went into creating it from nothing and you will have a good idea of your place on the pricing scale. So, you know that it is worth it.

If you are in a service business, you must realise that you are not being paid for a day or an hour of your time. You are being paid for the years of experience, skills, training, knowledge, capability and competency you built up to be able to do that job. You are also being paid for taking the risk of running a business that provides that service, which means that they don't have to employ people on stand-by to do that job.

By the time I was about to start charging, I had seen a lot of consultants come and go over the years. I saw some amazing ones, some mediocre and some who should have been frankly ashamed to take the money. There were some I worked with at top day rates that I knew were more experienced than me. I also knew that there were some who had broader experience than me. I knew that there were many who had as deep experience in project sponsorship and very few who had that plus international experience. So, I knew that was the most valuable experience that I had and would be the work I could charge the highest day rate for. I had no problem charging it and being paid because I had done a lot of work on self-worth. Plus, and here is one upside to being a workaholic, you always know you deliver value and that you get the work done.

What I want you to be honest with yourself about it is whether you really cannot figure out the right pricing or whether there is a little Gremlin in your head telling you that you are not worth it. Be honest with yourself because if there is a Gremlin in there, you must perform an eviction. Your business is not renting headspace to Gremlins. You are going to complete an eviction process.

The reason you must evict that Gremlin and not just ignore it is that, even if you silence him or her for now so that you can price the work, win it and earn all the money, it won't be the end. It will be Gremlins 2 – You're still not worth it. That's when you earn all the money and then make some Gremlin influenced choices about what you do with it. Over giving, risking it, hoarding it, getting into wild panics or just putting it in the bank and refusing to look at it. Think I am exaggerating? I know at least one entrepreneur who has done each of those things with money they earned that they didn't think they deserved.

I must tell you one last very important piece of information about pricing. You cannot ever approach someone else who is bidding for the same piece of work as you, ask them what they are going to bid and agree on prices. This is called price fixing. It is covered under different competition laws in the different countries where it applies, and it is illegal. If you even approach someone to start to suggest this, they may even be obliged to report you for this.

It is different from asking your competitors their general rates or an average day rate that you could expect to be paid. I will give you an example of the distinction.

I was approached by a client to submit a bid for some consulting work. He also told me that two other people were bidding. One, I knew, was a large consulting firm, so I knew their bid would be higher than mine. The other was someone I have known for years and worked with on and off. I knew there was a good chance he and I would both get the work. I called him to say that I heard we were both bidding and hoped we both got some work and would be delighted to work with him again if it did happen. What I could not ask him was what he would be charging as his day rate. He could not ask me either.

Fast forward to a year later and I was putting together a bid for another client and I had to submit a team. I called the same chap up and asked if he wanted to be in my bid and if so, what would his daily rate be. He told me, I added my fee to his rate and put it in the bid.

It can feel tricky talking with your peers about money and day rates but the difference in those two situations is that one would have been illegal and would have been in breach of anti-competition laws whereas the second was a simple part of me pricing a bid.

If we must bid against each other again in future I will of course know his day rates, but I cannot phone him back up and discuss in the context of a bid where we are separate bidders.

If you ever engage in price fixing it is a murky practice and you can be assured, it will be damaging to your business as your integrity and ethics will be in question forever. Price fixing is one of those business concepts that is quite easy to explain to the lay person so, unlike some complicated stuff that no one wants to report on, people get this one. It is a nice headline with your name under it. We have agreed you are quite exceptional, and I would like you to keep your exceptional self both in business and out of prison, so let's all agree to just not do it.

10

TAKE IT TO MARKET

W ell, what a great place you have arrived at now. You know what you want to offer, why, who you are going to offer it to, what it will cost. You understand that you are just as deserving as anyone to win the work and that you are worth every penny they are paying. You also have an amazing way to describe what you sell and articulate your offer from the elevator pitch to the boardroom slot.

You see, you are as amazing as I promised you.

What now? Well now you must tell all the people. Not just random strangers in the street. I mean, you can tell them if you like, go ahead, it's all practice but you may get a few strange looks. I am all of the view that other people's opinion of you is none of your business so from that perspective, it's fine, but it won't get you much corporate work.

You must take it to your marketplace. This we are going to look at in three styles. Individual, collective, and procurement lists

Individual

Let's look now at taking it to market on an individual basis. For that, we will head over to Hungary. How is your knowledge of Hungarian poets? Mine, I confess, is slim, neither deep nor broad. I know of one Hungarian poet and he is my current favourite. A chap called Frigyes Karintha.

You may not be overly familiar with his works, but you have probably heard of one of the concepts that arose from his short story, Chains. It is the concept of six degrees of separation. Karintha first mooted the theory that anyone on earth can be connected to any other person through a chain of acquaintances with no more than five intermediaries.

You may know a company you want to work with and think you have a barrier. That barrier could be that you do not know either the person you need to get your proposal in front of or anyone in that company.

But do you know someone who knows someone who knows someone? You can go to LinkedIn and have a look, as this will tell you up to three places how separate you are from someone. You might then be able to get that chain of connection to introduce you. You can also ask around.

 If you have decided you want to try to sell to A Big Company, tell people that and ask who knows anyone who works there. You will be surprised at how willing people are to help. I have introduced lots of people over the years who just got someone to approach me and say they wanted to put what they had in front of someone in one of the large corporates I worked at or with.

A few times, I have said it wouldn't be the right time as I have seen that their product or service isn't ready or isn't right for that company. Mostly, I have made the introduction. It doesn't guarantee you getting in the door, but it does massively increase the likelihood.

If you think that is too big a stretch, think of all those conversations over the years where you meet a new person and you start comparing lives and before you know it, you have a connection in common. You start saying what a small world it is. The world is massive and there are 7.8 billion people in it, but it is still amazing how interconnected we all are.

You are also going straight to your network here. In your list from Chapter 8 - Refine Your Strategy, who is on that list of people? You want to let them hear about your offer. So, go through that list and decide how you are going to do that?

- Tell them by phone,
- Ask to meet for coffee, lunch, dinner and tell them you want to share the details of your new offer with them?
- Give them a sample product?
- Send them a personalised message to view your website.

Now, what about the wider reach? Although you only have those six degrees of separation, you cannot invite the work out for coffee. The logistics alone are mind boggling.

So, consider how you will do some mass awareness:

- Email marketing campaign?
- Write an article about it on LinkedIn?
- Have a launch event?
- Send out email brochures
- Post out physical brochures?

I want you to feel comfortable doing this, so remind yourself that the gap in the middle exists, people in business impact other businesses to try to join their supply chain and sell to them. If you are doing this from a people first base, you are good to go.

Procurement lists

In your research, you may have come across useful information in the 'work with us' section of your chosen client's website. Did it say how you can apply for work that they put out to the marketplace?

If so, you want to subscribe to their list and start reading their emails and bidding for any work that you would like to win. If they host events such as meet the buyer, supplier events or market testing, then make sure you go along. The procurement teams will be there and it is a great chance for you to meet them, get to know them and start to build a relationship with them.

If they are in the public sector, they will be following the rules for the value and type of procurement they are putting out. I was going to include the value and categories here but as these change, I would have to re-write my book every time it changed. That hardly seems efficient. You would also have to buy a new copy every time and read it. That is not value for you. If you look on their websites or on the websites of the relevant government, you should be able to find these links easily enough.

These are the main sites that you want to be registered with. A word of caution. Choose your categories carefully and put a reminder in your diary to review them every quarter for your first year and then six monthly after that.

Unless you want to spend the rest of your work life down a procurement rabbit hole, I also suggest that you set up a procurement lists folder in your inbox. Then have sub folders for each procurement list. For each of the emails, set up an automatic rule that the emails go straight to the folder. Set aside half an hour or an hour every week or every two weeks to review these. The more you do it the quicker you will get at looking through them and figuring out if there is anything you want to bid on. Remember that writing and submitting a bid is a time critical process, so you should only start if you know you have the time to complete and really want to win and do the work.

Depending on the size of your business, you may want to hire someone to write bids for you or you may have an in-house person who can do this or can learn to do it. If you are outsourcing, make sure that you choose someone who understands the procurement rules and has written bids before. I work on these for myself and for clients and there is a particular approach that needs to be taken.

You are going to register on the relevant lists to get announcements about work opportunities. I do regular live sessions in my Facebook group about these lists, showing people how to figure out which ones you want to be on, which categories to select and how to manage this without getting completely overwhelmed.

Those lists will start to show you who is seeking what you sell. All the work on these is going to be awarded via a procurement process. This means that once you have decided that you want to go for one of them, you will have to submit a bid.

How long is a bid being the same answer as a piece of string. I have put in bids of 100 pages and bids of 6 lines of text.

Collectively

Trade shows

Now cast your mid back to Chapter 5. Remember those trade shows you used to find out a lot about your clients. Well, guess where you are going? Oh yes, like a modern-day Cinderella. you are off to the ball.

If you have a product, you want to be exhibiting that. You might also want to get a demonstration slot so that you can get on stage and talk straight to a group of buyers who want to see it in action.

If you have a service business, you can also choose to get a stand to exhibit. If you want to take that further, can you do a speaking gig at the show? Can you run a main workshop which gives enough of a taste or insight into what you do to showcase it and interest your potential clients?

If you have people come to your stand and chat to you from your target client, but they are not the right person, don't write them off. Can they make an introduction, pass on a brochure or can you help them right now, in that moment, with anything?

You might well get some introduction meetings set up. I have personally made a lot of introductions via events such as these. I have seen products or people that I knew someone else in my company or now, my client's companies, that I know they would be interested in and set up the introduction.

I have also met people who have then invited me into their companies to pitch my services to them.

Professional Institutions

Professional Institutions are another great place for you to take your offer to the market. There will be some obvious connections between certain corporate and professional institutes. For example, law firms are going to be members of The Law Society. Any property firm will be with the Royal Institute of Chartered Surveyors. These are UK based. Project firms will be with the Major Projects Association and / or the Association of Project Management in the UK or Project Management Institute in the United States and Canada.

Some corporates will be members of multiple professional institutes. Guess what? Your clients are hanging out there. When I was in corporate, this was where I knew my tribe would be. It was also necessary that I attended a set amount of continuous professional development in a year for any of the professional institutes where I was a registered member. I was in four at one point. That is a lot of events. That is a lot of places you can be putting on a workshop and displaying your offer right in my face. Or you can be attending and growing your network and telling me on an individual bias about what you do. It's a business-to-business environment so talking shop is appropriate and expected.

A word on emails.

When I worked in large corporates, I would get a lot of emails. I am an avid and a quick reader but there were times I would get 1250 or more emails every week, on top of a challenging job. Well, I did work 70-90 hours most weeks. Do you know how I managed to read them all? I didn't. Someone else did. My personal assistant would filter out anything that they deemed unimportant

If I said I was expecting a follow up from someone I met at an event, they would know to flag that for me or show me it and ask if I wanted to go ahead and have a follow up meeting. Requests for meetings with me would also be filtered by them. Let me tell you, they are the gatekeepers to senior leaders' diaries in corporate. This is good for you though, because they generally won't mess you around out of over politeness or awkwardness.

If PA says the diary is full that is usually the truth. If the answer is that hell will freeze over before you get to see this person because they have less than zero interest in hearing about your offer, then I think that is good news for you to hear. You can move on from that. If you love to punish yourself and really want to try to sell something to someone who does not want to see you, then best of luck to you and enjoy your punishment. Download yourself a lot of motivational posters about try, try and try again, read some books on persistence... Whatever you want really because although I am not going to say that you should give up at any hurdle in getting into corporate work, I am saying that a person who says they don't want to meet you to hear about your offer is either the wrong or the hardest route in. Be kinder than that to yourself.

Also, get your 1-minute, 3-minute, 10-minute and hour-long pitch ready because this is the phase of work where you are going to build your pipeline.

What is a pipeline?

This is a consistent flow of work into your business over the course of years. As you end one piece of work, you have others coming in. In the world of traditional marketing, the start of our pipeline is like a sales funnel.

You want to avoid having to win a piece of work, deliver it and go out and look for the next piece. That down time when you are looking for the next piece can be a bit longer in a business-to-business world because of the procurement process involved. So, either you end up doing lots of small pieces of work, generally under the £10k limit, or you are in the bid, wait, work, repeat phase. That is fine if you choose that but you risk fallow periods and must make sure you budget for that happening.

What you want is to be doing enough development, and attracting clients to work with you, that you have work in the pipeline that is secured. Have some prospective work that you are bidding for that happens within a date range. Have work that you are watching for bids coming out for and planning to meet the client and take them through what you offer with a potential to getting future work.

You want this to be a mix of existing and new clients.

How do you build a pipeline?

I use this system to plan and record.

Who do I want to have as Clients?

Current Clients & who else I want to work with now	Short term future clients (3-6 months)
Medium term future clients (6-20 months)	Long term future clients (20 months onwards)

Then I plan the actions that I am taking for each of those on the list relative to the stage they are at in my pipeline.

Current Clients & who else I want to work with now	Prospecting
Warming up	Raising awareness

The level of detail and certainty is more volatile the further out it is but you must always keep a watchful eye on how each aspect is coming along.

The great news is that when you are doing the work, sometimes a new or existing client will suddenly drip some work into your pipeline. Some work will come off and some won't.

How do you maintain a pipeline?

I plan actions every single month that reflect what is in these plans. Because it is planned and coordinated, it never gets overwhelming. I update my 12 months look ahead anytime there is a change, such as I win work, get asked to submit a proposal or get approached about work.

Also, if something interesting drops into my research box whilst I am sleeping about a company in the pipeline, it may mean that I choose to move them forward or backwards and take an action there and then. It could be as simple as call to say' I read x in the papers and wondered if you needed me to help by doing x, y or z'

Other than that, I do it every quarter. I look at how it is going, what is changing or maturing and whether I need to think about drawing in any more or any less.

How much to draw in at any stage?

This must be aligned to your vision of how much you need to make and how much you want to work. It is good to have more than you can do in your pipeline as sometimes, circumstances change and what you thought was a cert doesn't happen or the dates change. You do need to have a plan for what you will do if you win more work than you anticipated. Know when you are close to that happening by staying on top of your pipeline so that you reduce it to minimal overlap.

Does it ever run dry?

It will if you don't nurture it.

How much time to spend on it at the start?

This depends how big your business is and how big your existing network is. If no one knows who you are and what you do, then you could start with a full day or more every week to get it rolling. On average across the year, I spend about 2 days per month managing my pipeline.

How much to spend on it to keep it going?

It depends. This should be part of your project cost so CAPEX to set it up and OPEX to keep it running.

Work out what your budget is for this and review it annually.

Should you pay someone?

That is up to you. If you are your best asset and salesperson and you love doing it and can manage your schedule in a way that allows that, then I personally think that is the best way. You get a real feel for what is working and what is not working. People feel a strong connection to you as the business figurehead.

Hate talking to people or don't have time? You may want to think about a salesperson or sales team. You need to be sure that they do the work with your ethos and values at the front of every conversation they have with your potential clients.

You could pay a firm to trawl the procurement list for you and send you what you should bid for. There are several companies who will do that for you. I don't use any of them, but I get invited to bid for a lot for work and get invited to be part of other people's bids. If I wasn't and I needed to work and didn't have the time, I would consider it as an option.

The key to this is being a good client. Don't expect them to read your mind. Be very precise on the type of bids you want them to find you and if the first few they send aren't right, have a conversation with them and adjust as you go.

By following all of this advice and using a mix of getting onto frameworks, managing leads. Growing your network, being in bids, bidding for your own work, sourcing new clients and developing them, putting out marketing into the world, your pipeline will start to grow and flow.

Make sure you are keeping a good record of it as it makes it easier to allocate any spare time that you get to managing it as well as your regular planned time to work on it.

Never ever forget your existing clients. Your existing clients will bring you their work and be your best advocates. They are likely to have a network of people in their industry and will be happy to recommend or introduce you, but not if you work with them once and drop them like a hot potato.

One of the first decisions I make is once I have a new contract with a client, what will be my value-add that I will offer. I might not tell them straight away, but they will get it or experience it.

For example, I have a few clients who have had job interviews for promotions in the middle of me working with them. I have known that we are a good coaching match, so I have offered to do some coaching with them in preparation.

I have plenty of ongoing clients who know that they can call me and I will support them in that even when we are not working together because we have built an ongoing relationship.

Other clients have been mid recruitment and I have helped them source some candidates from my network.

Some I have done some extra hours on my consulting contract with them because I have seen that would be most useful to them.

Some clients I have brought in a specialist to do a short but powerful piece of work. I have paid the specialist but not billed it as an extra.

All of these have been good value adds to offer to existing clients. All are planned and strategic rather than just over delivering randomly.

You could say that putting on events is a value add for my clients. The relationship excels when they have a good time, and I can often introduce them to people like you, dear reader, and help close that gap in the middle. However, I feel that those events bring me in work, and I have such a good time just hanging out with people that I genuinely like. Being in host mode is something I relish (honestly, come to mine for a party, there might be geography chat, but you will be fed and watered and hosted so well, you won't want to leave) so it feels like I get as much out of it as anyone else. A great night with likeminded people and a few of your pals... what is not to like about that?

11

ETHICAL ENTERTAINING

By the stage that you need to consider how you will entertain clients, you either have corporate clients or you know who some of the individuals you want to have as corporate clients are. You are going to continue to do business with them and maintain a relationship. We are all agreed that relationships are the basis of all good work, aren't we?

Well, this is not a friendship in the purest sense of the word, so you are going to have to apply some rules to the relationship. Maybe that sounds awkward or formulaic, but it really isn't. Remember what I said in Refine your Strategy about your network? Ah yes, I hear you say. You told me not to force relationships or meet people thinking of my angle all the time. You said let the relationship be organic and genuine and now you tell me there will be rules and a structure.

You may well, dear reader, think that this is a contradiction and wonder whether I had two ghost writers and one ghosted me after chapter 8. The answer is no, I wrote all of this myself. And, yes, I did say it has to not be forced or so overtly self serving that you make it weird. That does not mean that we don't have some rules to follow.

When I first started working in corporates, I thought the rules around entertaining were weird, unnecessary and archaic. I don't mind admitting that there was some naivety in me back then that I wish was still there at times.

You see, I didn't think it was necessary as most humans are decent people who, given the choice, will do the right thing. And I mean consistently do the right thing, even when their circumstances change, or they are presented with opportunities for wrongdoing.

I even thought that after I had worked in the hospitality industry, which is one of the industries where pilferage is most rife and most difficult to control. I rationalised that a lot of the people doing the pilfering were under immense financial pressures.

I worked in an area that was in the midst of a heroin epidemic. A place with very high crime and dreadful poverty. Poverty isn't just about lack of cash or opportunity. Poverty is dehumanising and pushes shame and desperation into people's lives. Think that addiction is just a choice? Well, maybe the choice is more palatable when what you seek to escape is hardly bearable. I worked with people who stole cash, booze and sometimes food from the kitchens out of desperation. Working poor who had home circumstances I could see but not comprehend the depths of. I also worked with some thieves who just wanted to do it to get away with it. It opened my eyes but it did not make me change my view that most humans will make the right choice.

What changed my view was experience. Firsthand, up-close, full-frontal exposure TO corruption and inappropriate behaviour. In both the public and private sector. From people who could and should have done better.

There are plenty of articles written about these, so I won't go into the finer details here. The articles are written and published about those that have been proven. There are many others where the burden of proof has just not been met.

It would take someone with a more in-depth knowledge of psychology, human behaviour and group dynamics to explain why people do these things. The two traits that I have seen are greed and hubris.

So yes, the awkward rules do have to be in place. That means that you must learn them and then play by them.

You also have to keep up to date with any changes. I worked for a private company which became an arms-length body of government. Overnight, the rules on what hospitality and entertaining we could accept changed.

It meant a new set of rules for all our suppliers and for us. It was probably a year of rejecting invites and filling out the paperwork to say I had been invited and declined before everyone got familiar with it.

Some things are easy and apply everywhere. These include:

It is not appropriate to extend invites to anyone who might have influence over a bid or product acceptance once you are in the throes of it being assessed. I haven't worked anywhere that is seen as acceptable. Once in the assessment phase, you just don't do it.

There are times when the award of bids gets legally challenged and this could have a serious impact if it looked like you tried to wine and dine clients, mid assessment. It will also make you look inexperienced if you do this.

Extravagance is frowned upon, yet also contextual. For some, it is a cup of tea, for others, it is opera tickets, for others, it may be a yacht!

Family members awarding contracts to family is a public sector no – no.

Offering cash incentives for buyers to choose you. This is commonly known as bribery. You should be aware that if anyone asks you to pay them a bribe, in many countries you are legally obliged to report that to the authorities.

Threats or coercion

If you threaten or try to use information you hold or have access to in order to guarantee work is given to you, that will be threatening or coercion. This is also likely to see you fall foul of anti corruption or bribery laws.

I will offer you good counsel that if something feels inappropriate or you think if you saw it printed as a news headline it would feel difficult to defend, then just don't do it.

There are plenty of ways that you can ethically entertain new and prospective clients, whether they are in the private or public sector.

It is a huge part of building your network, building your relationships with people and managing your pipeline.

You want the energy, time and cost that you put into this to give you just reward, not make you look inexperienced or inappropriate.

What are the best ways to do this then?

Let's start with gifts

The UK public sector has as a rule about gifts with no nominal value. This is part of the Nolan principles, also called the seven principles of public life.

You can give a gift with no face value over £15. People tend to go for things like diaries, pens, mugs, office paraphernalia. These are good for spreading your logo and creating that reciprocity in the relationship that you will have read about in various sales and marketing books.

Some government departments will not accept anything, even a bottle of wine at Christmas. The details will be on their department website, so have a look at that.

I like a nice stationery item, but I find some of the corporate tat just nonsense. Five mints boxed and branded in a plastic container switch me right off. Sustainability is a strong value for me, so how sustainable is it to buy 100s of these which will be at landfill within a week?

You can choose what is right for your business, but I know that if I put those out, I would feel way-out of line with my values and my clients would raise their eyebrows!

Think carefully about gifts you want to have associated with you. One of my favourites I ever got given was a metallic card holder with my name inscribed. At that time, I was at industry events every week and I used it all the time.

The value would have been within what I could accept, so less than £15, and it met the criteria of no face value as an engraved card case with my name would be fairly tough to sell on.

Industry awards and events dinners are a good way to entertain your public and private sector clients. You can often buy a table or sponsor a part of the event, depending how much you want to spend. It will be a night out, aligned with you and your client's industry network and relevant speakers. A nice dinner and a chance to socialise. Plan out in advance which ones you want to go to, who you would invite and budget for these.

This can be a nice way of team and trust building in a more relaxed setting, but still professional.

You are also likely to meet other potential clients at these events but remember my word about existing clients; on these evenings they are your guest. Yes, you are taking them to dinner but they still chose to spend their time with you, and you cannot ignore them if you see a shinier prospect at another table.

When we brainstorm ideas for corporate events for our clients, I would say that 8 out of 10 ideas don't go ahead because it doesn't meet the 'looks, sounds and feels compliant' box. I never want my clients to feel compromised by me offering them anything inappropriate, so we are super careful.

It might sound cheap, but when we have an event that we invite government employees to, we tell them the cost per head so that they know we haven't gone over the value they would like to accept. I also know that it must meet the specific criteria for whichever government rules they have to follow, including departmental ones. I know that some government departments will just not accept anything at all, and I do not compromise them by asking.

None of this has to be undercover or secret service like. You can talk openly to clients or potential clients if you want to ask what their rules are. They are unlikely to feel awkward telling you.

It can become tricky when you are friends with some clients. I have known some of my clients over many years.

So how do you draw the line? Here is my imaginary line. Would I still see them if we were not doing business together? If we both won the lottery and never worked another day (this will not happen as I do not play the lottery, so perhaps if I write a bestseller one day instead) will I still call them up and chat? Those folks are my friends, my pals, my old muckers. If not, they are business contacts that I have a friendly relationship with.

You know what the great thing about your pals is? You can have an open discussion with them.

So that is what we do.

In the spirit of the rules?

There are so many things that you can do.

One of my favourite events we have held for clients was in 2021. It had been 18-months of events being cancelled, postponed or turning out to be super spreader events due to an attendee having covid.

A lot of my clients work in rail. If they are not in rail, it is likely that sustainability is important to them as that is such a strong value for me so I tend to attract clients like that. Every year, the Railway Benefit Fund has a raffle to raise money for the fund. That year one of the prizes was being driven around London for an hour on an old-fashioned red bus, driven by Sir Peter Hendy. Sir Peter is a transport celebrity as he was the Transport for London commissions before becoming the Chair of Network Rail. He was also undertaking some other prestigious roles.

I had worked for Network Rail when Sir Peter was Chair. He had asked me if I needed any help at one point. I had asked him to deliver a masterclass to the Directors of Sponsorship across the company. I asked him to talk to them about being in a leadership role and decision making when you are not sure what the right thing to do is and there is a lot of risk involved. Sir Peter had been the Commissioner at Transport for London during the London bombings. I knew he had to take the decision of when to switch all the London public transport systems back on after the terrible events of 2005. It was a huge decision for anyone to make and whilst you are surrounded by advisers of course, untimely you must take a decision based on risk and probability and live with the consequences of that decision.

He did the talk and whilst I can't share with you what he said, I can tell you that there were many times when everyone was speechless. Fast forwarding to 2021, I had seen him speak to large and small audiences a few times by then. I knew that my clients would love an audience with him type of event. The fact that the auction was also for a relevant charity to many of my clients made it a no-brainer. I bid for the event and I won it. The bus could hold 65 and would take them for an hour round central London. I arranged a date and planned to pick up and drop off next to Kings Cross Station. I also booked a private room at a pub in Kings Cross and put on some food and drink. I had to make sure it wasn't lobsters and champagne, as many of my clients work for the public sector, so I wanted to keep it under £30.

I could have thrown caution to the wind over the £30 because many of my clients would be able to demonstrate that the tour on a heritage bus, with a talk by a transport guru, was a relevant professional development opportunity and the networking would be valuable, however, I never want any of my clients to feel that they must worry or think too hard about whether it meets their ethics requirements. Staying within that limit is a really good way to do that.

When I sent out the invites, I let anyone in the public sector know that the value was £30 per head. It might sound like it devalues the trip but trying to make an event sound more than it is would only feed my ego, whereas letting them know that I understand what matters to them works, so it is customer focused.

As soon as the invites went out, I could see from the responses that people were up for attending. I invited along a bunch of people who I had been promising to introduce to each other throughout covid lockdowns.

For many, it was their first in person event for almost 2 years. For others, it was their first time in London for 18 months, having previously commuted there every day.

I invited the associates who work in my business and let them know that I was happy to introduce them to any of my clients that they hadn't met. The reason for this is that they also have their own businesses. Whilst you might think it odd that I would introduce people who could be my competitors to my clients, it really isn't. I only bring associates into my business who I know and trust. They all value collaboration as much as I do and none of us would ever do anything inappropriate. Plus, there are things that each of us is much better at than the other and we are likely to recommend each other for the work based on our strengths and experience anyway. I also told them that I would not be pitching, launching or announcing anything sales-y that night.

Although I was in the middle of creating a really exciting new digital product, I just did not want to do it that night. After the collective shock and trauma the world had experienced at that time, it felt wrong. Here I was, getting a group of superb people together for a nice evening and whilst they would have no problem listening whilst I did a 10-minute pitch, it just didn't feel right to me. I decided instead that I would say:

"Thank you everyone for coming. In a break with tradition, I am going to say very few words tonight. I wanted to have this event to bring together all my clients who have supported us since I started the business. I also want to thank all the associates too for all the hard work and dedication they have shown in working with clients. I often say the associates are like family and of course, as we do a lot of railway work, some of them are my family.

There is no sales pitch tonight, merely a thank you and enjoy your evening. You all do different things but the one thing that is common to all of you is that you do work that makes the world a better place. If we have learned anything over the last 18 months, it is just how important that really is."

There were a few misty eyes as it had been emotional for a lot of people to see each other after so long at home. There were some of us there who had only ever worked remotely with each other and were meeting in person for the first time. We had spent a lot of time in each others' lives through the strangest of times and it was nice to meet at last.

It felt like the right approach to leave out the sales. Now, I am not advising that you run events and don't even offer a sale to anyone who attends. That is not the message here. The message is that there are two areas you should consider in advance. One is what are their needs and the second is how will you balance those with your values.

If you value relationships above all else, then by stepping back from the sales at the right time to leave the focus on relationships, your business will thrive.

When I work with private sector clients, I know that they will have company specific rules on entertaining to follow. They may also have rules to follow specific to their field if they are in a regulated field of profession. I include it in my research work when I am looking at them as a potential client. Sometimes, the information is easy to come by. Sometimes it is not, or it is open to interpretation.

You know what is easiest? I just ask them. I tell them I would like to be able to entertain them or take them for dinner or drinks and I ask what the rules are.

The rules around corruption and bribery all still apply whichever sector you work with. In the Private Sector it is often the case that the limits on hospitality, and what is permitted as entertainment are broader.

That is not to say they are any less ethical than the public sector but they are not spending taxpayer's money in the same way; they do not have to abide by the 7 principles of public life. They also have company rules and governance in place relative to the structure and nature of the work they do, and it is entirely appropriate that they write the rules to reflect that.

This is the group of clients that you may have to offer a higher end experience to because that is what they will be used to but the same rules regarding what is completely inappropriate still apply.

This can be a fun part of corporate work. Spending time doing nice things with people you like working with and spending time with.

Getting it right from the offset so that everyone can enjoy it, planning it so that you can afford it and fit it in properly with enough time to really relax and enjoy it is the key. You see, I might not be able to do magic, but I can predict with certainty that your vision in Chapter 4 did not include 'feel so overwhelmed and stressed that I don't get to enjoy anything'.

You are going to investigate it, plan it, enjoy it and watch the relationships grow, your pipeline flourish and your visions come to life.

People are fine about sharing the information about what is permitted and what is not so don't be awkward or afraid to ask.

I will share with you a little story of how easy it is for a well meaning gesture to go awry.

It is important that you know what is allowed before you set off on buying gifts or inviting people to dinners or events.

It probably sounds like people could just decline but that simplifies the issue that people face in corporates. Whether public or private, there will be an ethics policy that they must comply with. There will also be anti-bribery and corruption rules to comply with, relative to their country.

Beyond that, there can also be a strong drive to 'look compliant' - that is to be seen to be complying.

This hit me big time in 2011. I was working with a large corporate. I had been negotiating a deal with a member of the public with his own business. He owned a popcorn factory. The deal was to buy the rights to one parcel of land he owned so we could put a railway through it instead of building a bridge between two parcels of land he owned. It was all heavily regulated and above board as it was public money we were spending. It took about 9 months of negotiations between the landowner and my company. My boss and I had several meetings to get a deal that worked and get it all approved.

When the deal was done, the man thanked us for the way we had conducted the negotiations. We were pleased at how it had all gone as these deals can get very emotional.

But then came the thank you gift from him! It was popcorn. It was a case of popcorn delivered to the building we worked in. That might seem innocuous to you ('it's popcorn, not Porsches. Calm down', you may say) but my boss and I were mortified. We had just struck a deal, had our company send a large cheque in settlement (which he was perfectly entitled to) and now there was a gift with our names on top of it and the logo of the popcorn factory owner on every side.

'The optics were not good' is as appropriate a corporate phrase as I can think of.

Two lawyers, the regional managing director, head of communications & media, my bosses' boss and a call to our client later, it was agreed that we could accept the popcorn, open it up at work and share it with staff at work. No taking any home, no tubs taken out to cinemas or folks' kids.

I had to phone the popcorn man to explain that we can't accept a personal gift, so we were sharing it. And to say thank you as he was just being kind.

It may seem dramatic but our ability to do our jobs and exercise the level of the decision making we had, relied on us being able to be impeccable. Any room for doubt when you manage public money is a career ender, rightly so.

Headlines of 'public fat cats scoff popcorn on YOUR money' tend to be damaging! It was a very public project and we were an organisation the public loves to hate.

It all blew over and we made a few jokes about going to prison for popcorn.

Although he had a business, it just hadn't occurred to him that we would be compromised so I share it as a cautionary tale.

A few years ago, the guy's son became well known for being on a reality show. My phone blew up with old colleagues messaging me telling me that popcorn guy junior was on the show. I did wonder if someone at the television or production company was in their reception, staring at a large case of popcorn thinking 'What am I meant to do now!'

12

CLOSING THE GAP

I hope that you realise that the time is now for you to take action. To follow all of the advice in this book and grow yourself a pipeline of corporate work.

You now know:

- Why you want to do to this
- How to go about it
- Where to start
- Who to contact
- When to start
- How to plan and keep on top of it
- That there are corporates just waiting to hear from you

You now have:

- A vision of what your amazing business and life will be like when you do this

- A way to implement and track your pipeline
- A reduced number of Gremlins and a way to evict any future Gremlins that try to make a home in your head
- All the information you need to start closing the gap in the middle

All of this is going to lead you into a wonderful life, designed by you.

You see, if a little girl from the poorest part of Glasgow can grow from there to have a multi 6 figure international business, working with huge corporates, then so, my friend, can you.

I have an amazing life, filled with genuine opportunities that I am truly grateful for.

ABOUT THE AUTHOR
CAROL DEVENEY

Carol is the founder and CEO of a global consulting firm, See Change International Consulting Ltd. She founded it after 20 years working in a variety of corporate environments. She has worked in logistics, hospitality, early years education, adult education, urban regeneration, employability, public transport and major projects.

Having studied business and run her own and other's businesses for so many years, she wanted to help small businesses achieve their goals of working in a business-to-business world.

As someone who has always embraced change, she enjoys helping others navigate through change towards positive outcomes. Whether that be building mega projects or helping small business owners stepping into more lucrative and secure work, change is her comfort zone.

Carol loves to help other business owners see that anything is possible for them and then help them plan the route to get there in a structured, strategic way.

She loves to travel and has lived in many cities, several countries and a couple of continents ....so far.

FREE HELP FOR YOU

I want this for you and I want to help you achieve it so you can get some free resources to help you here:

https://caroldeveney.kartra.com/page/Upw1#_32so1de7r

You can download my free guide '5 Things you need to know before you work with corporates' here:

https://caroldeveney.kartra.com/page/ZmG191

You can also join my free Facebook group for weekly practical advice

https://www.facebook.com/groups/entrepreneurs.getting.into.corporate

HOW YOU CAN WORK WITH ME

You can work with me on a consulting basis if you are a small business owner who wants to get into working with corporates or government organisations.

You can also join my group programme where you will be with other entrepreneurs on the same journey.

You can find more information on my website

www.caroldeveney.com

CONNECT WITH ME

You will find me on:

- facebook.com/caroldeveneycorporatestrategist
- instagram.com/caroldeveney_
- linkedin.com/in/carol-deveney

REFERENCES

Tony Buzan and Mind Mapping

https://tonybuzan.com/

Transit Maps of the World

https://www.penguin.co.uk/books/286/286645/transit-maps-of-the-world/9780141981444.html

ACKNOWLEDGEMENTS

I would like to thank Authors and Co for all of their help in making my dream to be a writer become a reality.

My husband, Brian, who always believes I can make anything happen and is willing to buckle in and join me on new life adventures wherever they take us. It's been a wild ride so far and we are nowhere near finished yet.

My son, Declan, who will never know how much his arrival changed my life for the better.

My family and friends who are my biggest cheerleaders and are too numerous to mention but you all know who you are. My people.

To all of my clients who put their investment of faith in me and my work. Know that I always find it a privilege and a pleasure to work with you.

Printed in Great Britain
by Amazon

82419617R00108